Sweet on Texas

Lovable Confections from the Lone Star State

SWEET
— ON —
TEXAS

★ **DENISE GEE** ★ **PHOTOGRAPHS BY ROBERT M. PEACOCK** ★

CHRONICLE BOOKS
SAN FRANCISCO

For Holly Dauphin Fields—
and the sweet memories of friends and family
who left us too soon.

Library of Congress Cataloging-in-
Publication Data available.

ISBN 978-1-4521-0248-1

Manufactured in China

Designed by Benjamin Shaykin
Food and prop styling by Denise Gee
Typeset in Deadwood, Hamilton,
and Titling Gothic

10 9 8 7 6 5 4 3 2 1

Chronicle Books LLC
680 Second Street
San Francisco, California 94107
www.chroniclebooks.com

ACKNOWLEDGMENTS

To Bill LeBlond and Amy Treadwell at Chronicle Books, and my literary agent Angela Miller—for helping make this book possible. Thanks for believing in me. And to the rest of the Chronicle Books team: Doug Ogan, Claire Fletcher, Alice Chau, Tera Killip, Peter Perez, and David Hawk, thanks for helping me look good. Thanks also go to copy editor Ann Rolke.

To Dale Dietert and Hank Hammett, two of the most creative, charming, and hospitable Texans I'm blessed to know. And to Pamela Elrod, whose stories of her aunt, Texas Elrod Culver (a.k.a. "Sugah"), and her family's East Texas farm named Plentywood, set me on my way.

To my brother Dempse McMullen, and friends Kirk and Joy Kirksey: Hats off for lending us some fab Texas wares for photography.

To my SMU colleagues in News & Communications: Thanks for putting up with my sugar rushes and helping me taste-test the goods.

To all those featured in the book who let me show off what *you* can do: Bless you.

To my mother, Freddie Lee, and father, Johnny—for letting me be born in this great state.

To my husband, Robert M. Peacock—a sweet soul and talented photographer—and Alfie the wonder dog: Thanks for being at my side.

Contents

Introduction

"Texas does not, like any other region, simply have indigenous dishes. It proclaims them. It congratulates you, on your arrival, at having escaped from the slop pails of other states."

—Alistair Cooke, legendary broadcast journalist (1908–2004)

Texans sport a self-assured lightheartedness that truly goes unrivaled. Our mostly rebellious country music says it all with a wide grin, but so, too, do our lesser-known ambassadors of attitude—our businesses. To wit, a billboard: "Walker Tires: If It's in Stock, We've Got It." A mattress store slogan: "Come to Us for the Best Lay in Town." On the door of a diner: "Warning: Unattended children will be given an espresso and a puppy." On the marquee of a quirky Mexican restaurant: "Show me on the doll where El Arroyo touched you." You just can't help but smile.

The Lone Star State has equal magnetism when it comes to food. There's our succulent brisket that we run smoke rings around compared to others; our ginormous chicken-fried steak slathered in peppery cream gravy; our Tex-Mex that's as American as fajitas. But one dining treasure often overlooked in the horn-tootin' department? Our desserts. Damn fine ones. Ones that represent our hospitality and sweetness like nothing else. Hence, this book. This is where I get to give Texas confections their moment in the sun. (Briefly, of course, before putting them back in the fridge. It gets hot here, y'all.)

Like Texas's topography, our desserts aren't easy to stereotype. That's because the state, which covers 268,601 square miles, is truly, as we say, "like a whole other country." There's a Southern drawl in the lush piney woods of our far east; the laid-back conviviality of Cajuns, Vietnamese, and "native Islanders" along the Gulf coast; the rich Mexican heritage of our festive border region; the free-spiritedness of our west's arid and mountainous Big Bend area; the artsy charm and eastern European heritage in the Hill Country; the rugged, old-Texas style of San Antone and El Paso; the cowboy and prairie flavors northward to the Panhandle; and the poshness of Dallas and Houston.

And though there's so much that differs, there are two things that bring us together: a friendliness that is unmatched and our love of fellowship, made sweeter as we sit down and enjoy dessert together. (Even the name "Texas" derives from the Caddo Indian word *tejas*, for "friends.")

This book is a collection of the very best desserts—not all of them, mind you, just some personal favorites—representing each of our four culturally distinctive regions: East/Coastal, Central, South, and North/West. It wasn't too hard to figure out where to draw the lines of demarcation, though of course they blur in spots, but not in others, which might surprise some people. Dallas and Fort Worth in two different chapters? You bet: Despite being only thirty miles apart, their styles and personalities couldn't be more different. Fort Worth really is where the East meets the West.

I must admit, the pressure was on while researching and testing these recipes. You see, like everything we do in this state, it better be good. It better be authentic. And it better, as folks might say, "cook right." For this I know: My fellow Texas foodies will be paying attention and will let me know about it if I'm not shooting straight.

Much of my research has been during the last four decades. I was born in Houston, and while I was raised in Mississippi, I regularly visited family in the Lone Star State before my husband and I ultimately anchored in Dallas after stints living in Galveston and Austin. Even while living in Birmingham, Alabama, and working for *Southern Living*, I traveled the state extensively, covering foodies and chefs for food features and also serving as the magazine's "Texas Living" editor. And then when I was managing editor of *Coastal Living*, I called the Texas food and travel beat. And even when I was a senior home design editor for *Better Homes and Gardens*, I called the Texas beat—even moving here to serve as its regional editor (thank you, BH&G). This place kept calling me back. I just had to stay put.

In keeping with our state's rich and engaging diversity of people and ingredients, *Sweet on Texas* features the must-know, must-eat recipes and must-meet dessert devotees from my own knowledge base as well as what's been graciously shared with me by the state's top restaurants and diners, home cooks, and bakeries. It dishes on each recipe's most interesting bit of history, technique, or ingredient. But its ultimate goal? To leave you, my kindred dessert-loving brethren—wherever you are—in an altogether other great state: of cold and creamy, warm and gooey euphoria, Texas style.

Now then. Enough yammering. Let's eat.

EAST TEXAS MEETS THE DEEP SOUTH

Texas is half South and half Southwest, with its eastern "Southern" drawl reflecting more of a honey y'all than a sassy twang. This is the land just past the Louisiana and Arkansas state lines, from Texarkana down to Dallas and continuing through Tyler and Houston, Beaumont and Galveston. This is the land of pine trees and blues music, St. Augustine grass and azaleas, swamps and gators, beauty queens and Mary Kay cosmetics, sweet tea and fried chicken, columned mansions and tin-roofed cottages, Caddo Lake up north and the Gulf down south, skyscrapers and NASA, chintz and damask, billionaires and bikers sitting side by side at a diner counter. Following is a virtual boo-fay of some of this region's favorite sweet things.

MAMA MARION'S MANDELBROIDT

MAKES 36 TO 48 COOKIES ★ I adore Three Brothers Bakery in Houston, not only because the family that owns it (and has for five generations) make dreamy pies and sweet breads, but also because, well, the place has soul. You can just feel it. Taste it. (What's more, the family never gives out its recipes, so having this one is a real treat.) This *mandelbroidt*, essentially a nut biscotti, hails from owner Janice Jucker's maternal great-grandmother, Chassi, who lived in Russia. Chassi died in a cellar while helping hide the czar's men during ethnic violence in the early part of the twentieth century. And on Janice's husband's side of the family, close family hid from the Nazis under the floorboards of their home. The entire family fled religious persecution to come to America. And the success that's followed just proves everything can't be taken away from a family. Memories and traditions live on through recipes.

MANDELBROIDT

5 cups sifted all-purpose flour

1 teaspoon baking soda

½ teaspoon salt

2⅓ cups packed light brown sugar

1 cup (2 sticks) unsalted butter, at room temperature

4 eggs

2 cups chopped pecans, walnuts, or almonds, toasted (see Note, page 30)

2 teaspoons almond extract

1 teaspoon vanilla extract

SEMISWEET CHOCOLATE GLAZE

1½ cups semisweet chocolate chips

6 tablespoons (¾ stick) unsalted butter

2 tablespoons light corn syrup

½ teaspoon vanilla extract

{ continued }

TO MAKE THE MANDELBROIDT: Preheat the oven to 350°F.

IN a large bowl, stir together the flour, baking soda, and salt.

IN another large bowl, combine the sugar, butter, and eggs. Stir until smooth and add to the bowl of dry ingredients; mix well. Add the pecans, almond extract, and vanilla; mix well.

USING floured hands (the dough will be sticky), roll the dough into three rounded logs, 2 to 3 inches wide, and bake on a parchment paper-lined baking sheet for 20 minutes. Remove from the oven and let cool for about 10 minutes.

REDUCE the oven temperature to 325°F.

USING a serrated knife, slice each log into 1- or 1½-inch sections. Place them on a parchment paper-lined baking sheet. Bake in batches for 10 minutes or until the cookies are firm. Remove and let them cool on wire racks.

TO MAKE THE GLAZE: Put the chocolate chips, butter, and corn syrup in the top of a double boiler over hot (but not boiling) water. When the mixture is melted and smooth, stir in the vanilla.

DIP half of each cookie in the chocolate glaze and let them rest, until the chocolate is firm, before serving.

NOTE: The cookies can be frozen for up to 6 months, layered in an airtight container with wax paper.

Divide and Conquer: Cookie Swaps

Cookie swaps or exchanges are the potlucks of dessert roundups, cleverly created so that members of small or even large groups can bake and take one batch and, after the party, wind up with maybe a dozen different varieties to enjoy during the holiday season.

In Galveston, the University of Texas Medical Branch has had twenty-five years of perfecting cookie swaps. Here's how they make it work:

★ Twenty people commit to each making ten dozen homemade cookies.

★ Each person then divides his or her cookies into twenty baggies of six, with the recipe affixed to each baggie.

★ One baggie is reserved for placing on the tasting table, where the cookies will be presented and discussed before being voted on for "best looking" and/or "best tasting."

★ After the event, each person goes home with a half dozen samples of nineteen different cookies.

★ Collect the recipes: They can be published in a keepsake cookbook that might be sold to benefit a charity.

Over the years the Galveston group has experienced sadness, like when one of their friends and fellow bakers died of leukemia. There's also been joy when another baker, Mary Bass, was inspired to start her own cake-ball business (and now Viva la Cake Balls is going gangbusters).

Through the decades, there have been hundreds of recipes enjoyed: pecan bars, chocolate macaroons, white chocolate chunk cookies, thumbprint cookies, gingersnaps, peanut brittle, and more. There have been traditional favorites, but also some ethnic varieties many might never be exposed to otherwise. The Chocolate-Peanut Clusters (page 18) and Cran-Pistachio Cookies (page 19) are two of their recent offerings.

CHOCOLATE-PEANUT CLUSTERS

MAKES ABOUT 60 CLUSTERS ★ Melanie Loving has been with the University of Texas Medical Branch cookie-swap group since its inception. "Being a part of it is the perfect way to outfit my holiday table with all types of cookies and candies," she says. In the case of this one, you only need your microwave to make it. Here's to her being one smart cookie.

One 1-pound package chocolate- or vanilla-almond bark

One 12-ounce bag milk chocolate chips

One 8-ounce can salted peanuts, or more as desired

MICROWAVE the almond bark in a microwave-safe bowl at high power for 3½ minutes (the bark will not lose its form). Remove and stir to melt the bark. Add the chocolate chips and stir. Add the peanuts and stir.

DROP the mixture by teaspoonfuls onto wax paper. Let them cool until they set. Store, covered, at cool room temperature for about 1 week.

CRAN-PISTACHIO COOKIES

MAKES ABOUT 48 COOKIES ★ The red and green elements are so festive, and because of the fresh flavors of cranberries and pistachios, you'd never know that these treats, made by Kim McInnis, were made with cookie and pudding mixes.

One 17.5-ounce pouch sugar cookie mix

One 3.4-ounce box pistachio instant pudding and pie filling mix

¼ cup all-purpose flour

½ cup (1 stick) unsalted butter or margarine, melted

2 eggs

1 cup dry-roasted salted pistachio nuts, chopped

½ cup dried cranberries, chopped

PREHEAT the oven to 350°F.

IN a large bowl, stir together the cookie mix, pudding mix, and flour. Stir in the butter and eggs until a soft dough forms. Add the pistachios and cranberries; mix well.

DROP portions of the dough, using a small cookie scoop or heaping teaspoon, 2 inches apart on ungreased cookie sheets. Press each scoop with your fingers to slightly flatten it.

BAKE 9 to 11 minutes, or until the edges are a light golden brown. Let cool for 2 minutes, then remove the cookies to a wire rack. Cool completely. Store tightly covered at room temperature for about 1 week.

DULCE DE LECHE BREAD PUDDING

SERVES 8 TO 10 ★ Texas's undisputed melting pot is Houston, where native Texans, Native Americans, Latin Americans, African Americans, Caribbean peoples, Vietnamese, Southerners, Yanks, and millions of others commingle culinarily with finesse. Here's an example of a cumulative creation, in this case featuring a lively mix of south Louisiana's liquored-up bread puddings, Latin America's rich dulce de leche, and the Caribbean's zippy rum. And when all this collides with vanilla bean ice cream? *C'est si bueno, mon.*

DULCE DE LECHE SAUCE

3 cups heavy whipping cream

3 cups packed dark brown sugar

2 cups sweetened condensed milk

BREAD PUDDING

Eight ½-inch-thick slices rich egg bread (such as challah, Hawaiian-style, or croissants), crust trimmed, cut into 1-inch cubes (about 10 cups)

4 tablespoons (½ stick) unsalted butter, melted

2 cups heavy whipping cream

4 eggs

2 egg yolks

3 tablespoons amber or dark rum

1 teaspoon vanilla extract

⅛ teaspoon salt

½ cup caramel bits or butterscotch chips

2 tablespoons light brown sugar

¼ cup powdered sugar

TO MAKE THE DULCE DE LECHE SAUCE: In a medium, heavy-bottom saucepan, combine the cream and sugar and stir over medium heat until the sugar dissolves. Gently boil the mixture until it reduces in volume by one-third, stirring occasionally, for 5 to 7 minutes. Stir in the condensed milk. Cover and refrigerate for at least 3 hours to ensure that the flavors meld.

TO MAKE THE BREAD PUDDING: Preheat the oven to 350°F.

PUT the bread cubes in a large bowl. Add 3 tablespoons of the melted butter to the bread; toss to evenly coat. Transfer the buttered bread to a baking sheet and bake until it begins to turn golden, 10 to 12 minutes. Remove from the oven and let cool.

COAT an 11-×-7-inch glass baking dish with the remaining 1 tablespoon butter and set aside. (Note: Glass dishes help you see how quickly a dish is browning.)

IN a medium, heavy-bottom saucepan, combine the cream with 1 cup of the dulce de leche sauce and stir over medium heat until it just begins to bubble. Remove from the heat.

IN a large bowl, whisk the eggs and egg yolks. Add the rum, vanilla, and salt. Slowly incorporate the warm dulce de leche-cream mixture. Fold in the bread cubes and refrigerate for about 30 minutes, gently stirring occasionally.

CAREFULLY fold the caramel bits into the chilled bread pudding mixture, so that the bread holds as much of its shape as possible. Transfer this final mixture into the prepared baking dish and sprinkle with the brown sugar.

BAKE for about 30 minutes, or until the mixture is set in the middle. Allow it to cool on a wire rack for 10 to 15 minutes and then dust with the powdered sugar.

IN a medium saucepan, slowly warm the remaining dulce de leche sauce over medium-low heat.

CUT the bread pudding into squares and serve warm with dulce de leche sauce.

SWEET TALK Latin-cooking purists know that true dulce de leche (meaning "sweet milk") is made with milk, sugar, vanilla, and baking soda—and takes hours of slow cooking to condense to impeccable richness. This version, however, saves loads of time and is equally delicious.

Use any leftover sauce on ice cream or atop fruit or cake. Or better yet, double the amount of sauce to ensure you can do just that.

JENAY'S FAMOUS LEMON BARS

MAKES ABOUT 20 SQUARES ☆ Jenay Benge may only be twelve, but she cooks like an old soul. Five years ago, the aspiring pastry chef won the attention of star chef Kevin Rathbun after she began baking to raise money to attend a Central Market cooking class in Dallas. Soon she and Kevin were exchanging cooking tips, and the next thing you know, Jenay's lemon bars were being served at his Blue Plate Kitchen. Published here for the very first time, these beauties are a perfect balance of sweet and tart. "They just taste like summer," she says. Here comes the sun.

2½ cups all-purpose flour

1 cup (2 sticks) unsalted butter, at room temperature

½ cup powdered sugar, plus extra for sprinkling

6 eggs

3 cups granulated sugar

1 cup fresh lemon juice

½ cup freshly grated lemon zest

1 teaspoon baking powder

PREHEAT the oven to 350°F and coat a 9-×-13-inch baking pan with cooking spray.

IN a large bowl, stir 2 cups of the flour together with the butter and powdered sugar to make a dough. Spread the mixture into the prepared pan, building up a 1-inch edge on all sides.

BAKE for 15 minutes, until very lightly browned; remove from the oven and place the pan on a wire rack. (Leave the oven on.)

IN a large bowl, use an electric mixer to mix the eggs with the granulated sugar, lemon juice, and lemon zest; set aside.

IN a small bowl, mix the remaining ½ cup flour with the baking powder. Add the flour mixture to the egg mixture and mix well.

POUR the mixture over the prebaked crust.

BAKE for 25 to 30 minutes, or until golden around the edges and set in the middle. Let the bars cool on a wire rack for 10 minutes before refrigerating for another 30 minutes (which makes them easier to cut). Cut into squares and sprinkle with powdered sugar. You can eat them warm or at room temperature, but I love them ice-cold.

{ continued }

STORE the bars, covered in plastic wrap, at room temperature for a couple of days (but they will best retain their flavor and shape for about 1 week in the refrigerator). They also can be stacked on layers of wax paper and frozen for about 1 month. Thaw them in the refrigerator.

SWEET TALK A half cup of lemon zest? When most recipes call for only a tablespoon or two? Wouldn't the tartness annihilate your taste buds? Nada. Jenay's figured out just the right balance of deep lemon and soft sugar flavor.

Dustup Dress-Up

Powdered sugar is fluffy and pretty and all, but let's face it—it's messy to handle. And since sifters—a necessity for making the sugar even finer than it already is—are a must but often look so utilitarian, let's try a trick my grandmother used: decoratively serving spices in small baby-food jars. In this case, though, we'll use a glass canning jar. Cut a piece of parchment paper into about a 4-inch square, trimming the edges decoratively with craft scissors, if you'd like. Place the paper atop the powdered sugar–filled jar. Screw on the ring, omitting the cap. Use a wooden skewer to poke holes in the paper. Serve it alongside a dessert to let people add even more goodness to their goodie.

THE MANSION ON TURTLE CREEK
RASPBERRY BROWNIES

MAKES ABOUT 16 BROWNIES ☆ Life may be sweet in Texas, but it's especially so for our forty-seven billionaires. According to Forbes.com, seventeen live in the Dallas–Fort Worth area, and twelve in the Houston region. And when most people picture folks with big money in DFW, they often think of them with big hair and big personalities. The latter is nearly always true. But as for that big hair: With the exception of a few of the city's highly teased and well-preserved grand dames, that coiffing trend has delightfully departed from the Big D. The folks with big personalities and big money always make their way to the Mansion on Turtle Creek. It's there that you can not only rub egos with the city's most beautiful people, but also enjoy some exquisite French-meets-Texas fare. This dessert is as elegant and simple as the new Dallas chic—and rich in its own way.

MARINATED RASPBERRIES

48 large or 64 small fresh raspberries (about 1 pint)

1 cup raspberry liqueur (Chambord or Mathilde Framboise)

1 cup sugar

1½ cups water

1 vanilla bean, split and scraped, or 1 teaspoon vanilla extract

BROWNIES

1¼ cups unsalted butter, melted

2¼ cups sugar

1 tablespoon vanilla extract

6 eggs

1½ cups sifted pastry flour (see Note)

1 cup cocoa powder

½ teaspoon salt

½ teaspoon baking powder

CHOCOLATE GANACHE

⅔ cup heavy cream

⅔ cup corn syrup

½ tablespoon vanilla extract

2 egg yolks

1⅓ cups chopped 55% to 65% dark chocolate

½ cup unsalted butter, softened

Garnish: 16 fresh raspberries, lightly dusted with sifted powdered sugar

{ continued }

TO MAKE THE MARINATED RASPBERRIES: In a medium mixing bowl, gently combine the raspberries and liqueur and set aside. In a small saucepan over medium heat, combine the sugar, water, and vanilla bean seeds and pod and bring to a boil, stirring occasionally for about 5 minutes. Remove from the heat, pour the mixture over the raspberries, and let cool. Cover and refrigerate overnight (to ensure fullest flavor) or for at least 6 hours.

TO MAKE THE BROWNIES: Preheat the oven to 350°F and grease and flour (or line with parchment paper) sixteen 2½- to 3-inch round dessert molds (see Note). In the bowl of a stand mixer fitted with the paddle attachment, beat the butter, sugar, and vanilla at medium speed until smooth and creamy. Add the eggs, one at a time, beating after each addition until fully incorporated. In a large bowl, sift together the flour, cocoa powder, salt, and baking powder. Add the dry ingredients to the wet ingredients a little at a time, stirring after each addition until well combined.

POUR the batter into the prepared molds. Place 4 marinated raspberries (reserving the liquid) on top of each brownie (if the berries are large, you may need only 3).

BAKE for 22 to 24 minutes, until the brownies are set and a toothpick inserted in the center of a brownie comes out clean. Remove to wire racks. While the brownies are still warm, drizzle 1 tablespoon of the reserved raspberry marinade over each brownie, and let the brownies cool completely; remove from the molds.

TO MAKE THE GANACHE: In a medium saucepan over medium heat, combine the cream, corn syrup, and vanilla and bring to a boil. Remove from the heat. Add the egg yolks to a large bowl and add the cream mixture in a slow steady stream, whisking constantly to temper. (You may need an extra set of hands.) Return the mixture to the saucepan.

{continued}

ADD the chocolate pieces to the mixture and let sit for 2 minutes, then whisk until smooth. Add the butter and blend into the mixture using an immersion blender (this is important because the ganache will appear "broken" if not properly mixed). Let cool.

FROST the brownies with the ganache and garnish each with a powdered sugar–dusted raspberry. Store in an airtight container in the refrigerator for up to 1 week.

NOTE Pastry flour (with 8.5 to 9.5 percent protein) is a softer product than all-purpose flour (10 to 12 percent protein), but it's not as soft as cake flour (7 to 8.5 percent protein). It can be found in most major supermarkets and specialty grocers or ordered online. The Mansion and I both favor the beautifully stone-ground products made at the historic Homestead Gristmill near Waco (see Sources, page 200). If you don't have pastry flour on hand, the rule of thumb is to substitute 1 cup all-purpose flour for ½ cup cake flour.

If your kitchen, like most, isn't outfitted like a bakery, with dessert molds aplenty, use three 6-mold mini cheesecake pans with removable bottoms (see Sources, page 200). You also can use jumbo muffin pans, but make sure you use parchment paper to ensure easy removal, and fill each tin only halfway (you don't want the brownies to get a "muffin top," because their delicate texture makes a thin rim prone to breaking apart).

SWEET TALK Save the leftover raspberry marinade to use in iced tea and cocktails. *De-lish*. Stored in an airtight container, it will keep nicely in the refrigerator for about 2 weeks.

LOADED PECAN TASSIES

MAKES 48 BARS ⋆ Bourbon. It does a pie good. Or at least that seems to be the case in the wilds of Texas, where pecan trees proliferate. Some pecan pies *look* tasty, but they're what President Lyndon B. Johnson might have called "all hat and no cattle." With these little tarts, the bourbon adds the cattle. The chocolate adds even more. I love the make-aheadness of these (see Note), as well as their easy-to-eat size, especially for parties.

1 cup (2 sticks) unsalted butter, at room temperature, plus 2 tablespoons melted

8 ounces cream cheese, at room temperature

2½ cups all-purpose flour

1½ cups packed brown sugar

1½ cups chopped pecans, lightly toasted (see Note)

⅔ cup milk chocolate chips

2 eggs

3 tablespoons good bourbon

IN a large bowl, beat the 1 cup butter and the cream cheese at medium speed with an electric mixer until creamy, about 30 seconds. Gradually add the flour to the butter mixture, beating at low speed until well combined.

SHAPE the mixture into 48 balls about 1½ inches in diameter and place them on baking sheets, not touching and covered with plastic wrap; refrigerate for at least 1 hour or overnight.

PREHEAT the oven to 350°F. Lightly grease two mini-muffin pans (each with two dozen cups) with butter or baking spray and set aside.

PLACE one dough ball into each muffin cup, shaping them into tart shells.

IN a medium bowl, whisk together the brown sugar, pecans, chips, eggs, bourbon, and 2 tablespoons melted butter. Spoon into the tart shells to fill them two-thirds full.

BAKE for 20 minutes, or until the filling is just set. Cool in pans on wire racks for about 15 minutes. Remove the tassies from the pans; cool on wire racks until completely cool. Store in an airtight container in the refrigerator for up to 1 week.

{ continued }

NOTE Toast nuts in a baking pan for 5 to 8 minutes at 350°F. Watch carefully to prevent burning.

Make these ahead and freeze them in airtight containers lined with wax paper; defrost in the refrigerator overnight or at room temperature a couple of hours before serving.

SWEET TALK "The pecan is a native nut that finds its way into just about everything, sooner or later. We have to laugh when we think of pecans, because we are reminded of one of the mild disagreements between the early Anglos and the friendly Tonkawas ... hired by the settlers to gather pecans from the trees on the farms, a process that normally involves threshing the limbs with long slender poles. The Tonks, being a practical people, decided that the quickest and therefore most profitable way to gather pecans was to cut the limbs off the trees." —*The Texas Cookbook: Culinary & Campfire Lore from the Lone Star State*, by Arthur and Bobbie Coleman, 1949

COCONUT DREAM PIE

MAKES ONE 9-INCH PIE ✭ For Dallas restaurateur and big ol' teddy bear of a guy Shawn Horne, being a grandmama's boy set him on the path to livin' (and workin') right. His Oma was especially adept at conjuring up dense, velvety custards, like the one in this decidedly voluptuous coconut cream pie. "Because the custard was so smooth, I was fed this as early as age six months," Shawn says. "Then, because I loved it so much, it was my 'birthday cake' all through my youth." The white chocolate brushed onto this piecrust is a hidden surprise and gives it the Dallas-dandified treatment. Not hidden is his use of freshly toasted coconut flakes, which gives this added grandeur.

2½ cups milk

⅔ cup granulated sugar

½ teaspoon salt

½ vanilla bean

7 egg yolks

½ cup cornstarch

5 tablespoons unsalted butter, cut into small pieces, at room temperature

1¾ cups coconut flakes, toasted (see Sweet Talk)

2 cups heavy whipping cream

½ cup powdered sugar

1 ounce white chocolate

One 9-inch prebaked Butter Pastry pie shell (page 168)

IN a medium heavy-bottomed saucepan, combine the milk, ⅓ cup of the granulated sugar, and the salt. Split the vanilla bean and scrape the seeds into the pan, discarding the pod. Mix well and cook over medium-high heat, stirring occasionally, until the vanilla-milk mixture just begins to boil.

IN a medium bowl, whisk together the egg yolks and the remaining ⅓ cup granulated sugar until well combined. Add the cornstarch, ¼ cup a time, and whisk until the eggs are thick and pale.

POUR a very small amount of the hot milk mixture into the egg mixture, whisking constantly. Very slowly add the remaining milk mixture into the egg mixture, whisking steadily until thoroughly combined. Return the milk-egg mixture to the saucepan. (If for some reason it clumps a little, strain the mixture and return it to the saucepan.)

COOK the custard over medium-low heat, whisking constantly to ensure a smooth texture. When the mixture begins to thicken (after 18 to 21 minutes), reduce the heat to low and stir quickly until the mixture takes on a pudding consistency.

{ continued }

REMOVE the pudding from the heat and pour it into a medium bowl set in an ice bath, which will help stop the cooking process. After the mixture has cooled a bit (about 15 minutes), stir in the butter and mix well. Stir in 1¼ cups of the coconut flakes.

PRESS a sheet of plastic wrap against the surface of the custard to prevent a skin from forming atop it. Refrigerate it for 3 to 4 hours, or until well chilled.

IN a chilled metal bowl, whip the cream (with cold beaters) with the powdered sugar on high power for 2½ to 3½ minutes until soft peaks form; keep refrigerated until ready to use.

IN the top of a double boiler, melt the white chocolate over barely simmering water.

BRUSH a layer of melted chocolate into the prepared pie shell. Spoon the chilled custard into the pie shell. Top with the whipped cream and the remaining ½ cup coconut flakes.

REFRIGERATE it for at least 4 hours before serving.

SWEET TALK To toast your own coconut flakes, preheat your oven to 325°F. Use a vegetable peeler to shave flakes from a freshly shelled coconut and spread them in a single layer on a nonstick baking pan. Cook for 12 to 15 minutes, or until the edges are just golden. Cool before sprinkling onto or into your confection.

RIGHTEOUS **RED VELVET** CAKE

MAKES ONE 8-INCH THREE-LAYER CAKE ★ This ruby-red chocolate cake has been my birthday cake of choice for as long as I could request it and have my way. And though I'm smitten with cream cheese frosting, I find more woo factor in the visual contrast between this cake's red and white layers, which is why I like to serve mine to highlight just that. This cake is as Southern as Southern can be, for sure, and in East Texas, it's a true taste of home. I get a little emotional each time I enjoy it, thinking of all the times I celebrated my birthday on Caddo Lake, which used to be pristine but is now struggling to be preserved. Long may it—and all of us—live.

RED VELVET CAKE

½ cup (1 stick) unsalted butter, at room temperature

1½ cups granulated sugar

2 eggs

2½ cups cake flour

2 tablespoons unsweetened cocoa powder

1 teaspoon baking soda

½ teaspoon salt

1 cup buttermilk

Two 1-ounce bottles red food coloring

2 teaspoons vanilla extract

CREAM CHEESE FROSTING

1 pound cream cheese, at room temperature

1 cup (2 sticks) unsalted butter, at room temperature

3 cups powdered sugar, or more as needed

2 teaspoons vanilla extract

Garnish: Fresh blueberries (optional)

{ continued }

TO MAKE THE CAKE: Preheat the oven to 350°F and grease and flour three 8-inch round cake pans. Set aside.

IN the bowl of a stand mixer fitted with the paddle attachment, beat the butter at medium speed until creamy. Gradually add the granulated sugar, beating until light and fluffy. Add the eggs, one at a time, beating just until blended after each addition.

IN a small bowl, combine the flour, cocoa powder, baking soda, and salt. Add them to the butter mixture alternately with the buttermilk, beginning and ending with the flour mixture. Beat at low speed just until blended after each addition. Stir in the food coloring and vanilla.

SPOON the batter into the prepared pans.

BAKE for 15 to 17 minutes, or until a toothpick inserted in the center of a cake comes out clean.

COOL the cakes in the pans on wire racks for 10 minutes. Remove from the pans to wire racks, and let completely cool.

TO MAKE THE FROSTING: Beat the cream cheese and butter at medium speed with an electric mixer until creamy. Gradually add the powdered sugar, beating until fluffy. Stir in the vanilla.

SPREAD frosting between the cooled cake layers and on top of cake and on the sides, if desired. Top with blueberries (if using). Store the cake at room temperature beneath a cake cover if planning to eat within a day, or in the refrigerator, tented with plastic wrap, for up to 3 days. Let the cake return to room temperature (this takes about 1 hour) before serving.

SWEET TALK A fun school of thought about what's essentially a devil's food cake is that the red coloring was added way back when to make it look, well, more devilish. That story's more fun than the likely reason: that the coloring was added to replicate the reddish color produced by old-fashioned ("un-Dutched") cocoa powder.

DOLLED-UP SWEET POTATO POUND CAKE

MAKES ONE 10-INCH CAKE ★ Most pound cakes are pure and simple. Pure butter, sugar, and flour. No frills. But sometimes a girl grows weary of wearing the same ol' tired dress. That's why this one's dolling up for today's occasion. There's sweet potato for richness, depth, and color, plus the delicious accessories of cinnamon and nutmeg, pecans, and chocolate. For even more decadence, give this girl some praline-flavored pecans and coconut flakes after glazing. But don't get too crazy, or she'll look like a floozy. On occasion I add a few tablespoons of bourbon while creaming the butter. But I just didn't want to have you meet this girl drunk without a proper introduction.

POUND CAKE

3 cups all-purpose flour

2 teaspoons baking powder

2 teaspoons ground cinnamon

1 teaspoon ground nutmeg

½ teaspoon baking soda

¼ teaspoon salt

1 cup (2 sticks) unsalted butter, at room temperature

1½ cups granulated sugar

½ cup packed light brown sugar

1 teaspoon vanilla extract

2½ cups cooked, mashed sweet potatoes (about 1¾ pounds) (see Note)

4 eggs, at room temperature

¾ cup chopped pecans

BITTERSWEET CHOCOLATE GLAZE

1 cup bittersweet chocolate chips

¼ cup (½ stick) unsalted butter

2 tablespoons light corn syrup

½ teaspoon vanilla extract

{ continued }

TO MAKE THE CAKE: Preheat the oven to 350°F and grease a 10-×-3½-inch Bundt pan.

IN a medium bowl, sift together the flour, baking powder, cinnamon, nutmeg, baking soda, and salt.

IN the bowl of a stand mixer fitted with the paddle attachment, cream the butter, both sugars, and vanilla at medium speed until light and fluffy. Blend in the mashed sweet potatoes, then the eggs, one at a time. Set the mixer speed to low and add the flour mixture in three batches. Combine until just blended. (The batter will be stiff.)

USING a spatula or wooden spoon, add the batter to the prepared pan.

GENTLY press the pecans into the top of the batter.

BAKE for 50 to 60 minutes, or until a toothpick inserted in the center of the cake comes out fairly clean.

TRANSFER the pan to a wire rack to cool (about 15 minutes).

INVERT the cake onto the rack and remove it from the pan.

TO MAKE THE GLAZE: In a double boiler over hot but not boiling water, melt and blend the chocolate chips, butter, and corn syrup. When the mixture is smooth, add the vanilla.

DRIZZLE the glaze atop the cake as desired before serving.

NOTE To mash sweet potatoes, peel and quarter the sweet potatoes. Add to boiling water and simmer, uncovered, until tender (about 20 minutes). Drain and mash.

SWEET TALK "Do not undertake any pound cake . . . unless you have the freshest and finest of eggs and butter." —*The Texas Cookbook: Culinary & Campfire Lore from the Lone Star State*, by Arthur and Bobbie Coleman, 1949

Sweet Potato Smash: Gilmer's Yamboree

When Texas counties were asked to celebrate what made them special during the Texas Centennial in 1936, Upshur County in the northeast Texas Piney Woods honed in on its hearty sweet potatoes and began celebrating them with a jamboree, er, "yamboree." And though the good people of Gilmer (pop. less than five thousand) aren't prone to calling their sweet potatoes "yams" like the more northern and western regions of our country, "sweet potato 'boree" just didn't have the same ring to it. For four days each October, one hundred thousand people converge on the town for a barn dance, tater trot, yam pie contest, fiddler contest, art show, queen coronation, and much more. By the way, this town's got soul: It's the birthplace of Freddie King, Johnny Mathis, and Don Henley.

MINT JULEP FRUITCAKE

MAKES ONE 9-INCH CAKE ☆ It's time to give the poor fruitcake a break. I, for one, have belittled them over the years because the ones I've had run-ins with have been hard as a brickbat and reeked of cheap rum. But after tasting a few good ones, I set out to create a really great one (at least to my mind—but of course, it could just be the bourbon talking). This white fruitcake is gorgeous baked in a fluted Bundt pan. The hole in the middle is just perfect for a small bouquet of fresh mint.

FRUITCAKE

4 cups candied pineapple bits

3 cups golden raisins

2 cups bourbon

2 cups (4 sticks) unsalted butter, at room temperature

3 cups powdered sugar

8 eggs

2 teaspoons mint extract

3 cups all-purpose flour, sifted

BOURBONY MINT SYRUP

1 cup water

½ cup granulated sugar

3 cups loosely packed fresh mint leaves

1 cup bourbon

Garnish: Fresh mint sprigs, powdered sugar

TO MAKE THE FRUITCAKE: In a large zip-top plastic bag, combine the candied pineapple, raisins, and bourbon and refrigerate for at least 3 days, stirring or massaging the bag occasionally.

PREHEAT the oven to 275°F and grease a fluted 9-×-3-inch Bundt pan. Place a small pan of water on the lowest rack of the oven.

IN the bowl of a stand mixer fitted with the paddle attachment, beat the butter and powdered sugar at medium speed until smooth and creamy. Stir in the eggs, one at a time, and mix until combined. Add the mint extract and the fruit-and-bourbon mixture. Add the flour, 1 cup at a time, and mix on low speed until combined.

FILL the prepared Bundt pan two-thirds full. Bake for about 2 hours, or until golden brown and mostly firm (until a toothpick inserted in the center of the cake comes out fairly clean). Remove the cake pan to a wire rack to cool for about 20 minutes.

TO MAKE THE SYRUP: Combine the water and granulated sugar in a medium saucepan over medium heat; stir until dissolved. Bring to a boil and add the mint leaves, submerging them completely. Remove from the heat, cover and let steep for at least 30 minutes.

STRAIN the syrup mixture through a fine-mesh sieve or coffee filter and let it cool. Combine it with the bourbon in a sealable container. If made ahead, keep it well chilled in the refrigerator.

POKE holes in the cake and pour in the mint syrup. Let the cake cool in the pan for another 20 minutes. Refrigerate it in the pan for 24 hours before removing the cake to a plate or tin lined with cheesecloth coated with some of the mint syrup (or just bourbon, if desired), to keep the cake moist. Before serving, garnish with powdered sugar and mint sprigs, if desired.

SWEET TALK "The fruitcake is the queen of the Christmas table. Beyond sensible question, it is the richest, most pleasing to the most people, and generally most satisfying of all cakes. And in contrast to more delicate cakes, it is one of the easiest to make." —*The Texas Cookbook: Culinary & Campfire Lore from the Lone Star State*, by Arthur and Bobbie Coleman, 1949

DEEP-FRIED COKE

MAKES ABOUT 36 BALLS ☆ Since Abel's recipe is a secret, this comes pretty dadgum close to what he invented in 2006—a concoction of fried Coca-Cola batter that sold 10,000 cups in just two weeks.

3 eggs

2 cups Coca-Cola

¼ cup granulated sugar

3 to 4 cups all-purpose flour

2 teaspoons baking powder

½ teaspoon salt

Vegetable oil for deep-frying

Powdered sugar

Pure cola syrup (see Sources, page 200)

Garnish: Whipped cream (optional), maraschino cherries (optional)

IN a large bowl, beat the eggs, then add the Coca-Cola and granulated sugar.

SIFT 2 cups of the flour, the baking powder, and salt and add to the Coca-Cola mixture. Mix while adding more flour, until the batter is smooth and not too thick.

HEAT the oil to 375°F in a deep fryer.

DROP 1½-inch dough balls into the fryer and cook for 2 to 3 minutes, until golden. Remove them with a slotted spoon to paper towels to drain.

SPRINKLE the fried Coke balls with powdered sugar while they are still hot, and douse with Coca-Cola syrup. Garnish with whipped cream and maraschino cherries, if desired, and serve.

Fried and True: The State Fair of Texas

At the annual State Fair of Texas (BigTex.com), which attracts three million visitors and is usually held late September through October, food and sticks go together like peanut butter and jelly (preferably fried, of course). Though other states come close to matching our moxie, we make bigger headlines for the likes of fried PB&J, fried pralines, fried cookie dough, fried banana splits, chicken-fried bacon, deep-fried butter, and fried Coke that compete for "best taste" and "most creative" during the Big Tex Awards. The undisputed king of the frying kingdom is Abel Gonzales ("the Willy Wonka of the State Fair of Texas," sayeth Andrew Zimmern of TV's *Bizarre Foods*). Abel has been so successful that he quit his day job of fourteen years (he was a computer programmer) just to keep the creative juices flowing alongside a small army of family and friends. Okay, tummies: Start your engines for this one.

TEXAS TWISTER (CHOCOLATE-ORANGE) MARSHMALLOWS

MAKES ABOUT THIRTY 1½-INCH MARSHMALLOWS ☆ Rachael Companik, who lives just north of Houston with her husband and three young daughters, is a marshmallow devotee, to say the least. She makes dozens of creative varieties (think chocolate-cherry, caramel–sea salt) to share with friends and family. "I've loved marshmallows of all kinds since I was a little girl. Even Peeps and the freeze-dried things from hot chocolate packets," Rachael says. But a few years ago she discovered the holy grail of marshmallows: homemade ones. As she puts it, "There's simply nothing else that compares to their tender perfection." Amen, sister. This recipe is insanely easy to make, and it's my new go-to recipe when I'm asked to bring a dessert I know will be easy to eat and everyone will think is fun.

2 cups granulated sugar

⅔ cup light corn syrup

Three ¼-ounce packets unflavored gelatin

¼ teaspoon salt

½ cup semisweet chocolate chips

2 teaspoons orange extract

2 to 3 drops natural orange food coloring (optional)

½ cup powdered sugar

½ cup cornstarch

PREPARE an 8- or 9-inch square baking dish by lining it with a sheet of plastic wrap, allowing the edges to hang over; coat with cooking spray with flour. Set aside another piece of plastic wrap, also coated with cooking spray.

IN a medium, heavy-bottomed saucepan, combine the granulated sugar, corn syrup and ¼ cup water and cook over medium-low heat, stirring occasionally.

ADD ½ cup cool water to the bowl of a stand mixer and sprinkle the gelatin and salt over it in order to soften the gelatin; stir to combine. Let it sit for at least 3 minutes.

{ continued }

ALLOW the corn syrup mixture to boil for about 1 minute, then pour it into the bowl of gelatin. Immediately beat the mixture with the whisk attachment on high for 12 minutes, until it has become thickened, white, and tripled in volume.

IN a small, heavy-bottomed saucepan or the top of a double boiler (or in the microwave for 90 seconds), melt the chocolate chips. Set aside and keep warm.

ADD the orange extract during the final minute of beating the marshmallow mixture. Turn off the mixer and add the food coloring (if using) and the melted chocolate. Mix slowly to create a marbled effect throughout the batter. (You may want to do this by hand to ensure you get the marbling effect you desire.)

USE a spatula to scrape the contents of the bowl into the prepared baking dish. Place the second piece of greased plastic wrap on top to cover it completely and pat it down to smooth the top and avoid creating a film.

LET the marshmallow mixture sit at room temperature for several hours or overnight to set. Remove it from the pan to a greased cutting board (it should come out of the plastic wrap with ease).

IN a shallow pan or on a plate, combine the powdered sugar and cornstarch.

USE a sharp, straight-edge knife to cut the marshmallow slab into desired shapes and sizes and lightly roll each in the sugar-cornstarch mixture to prevent sticking. (The marshmallows will look powdery for an hour or so before absorbing the sugar mixture.) If the marshmallow sticks to the knife, coat the knife in the sugar-cornstarch mixture or lightly oil it.

STORE for up to 2 weeks at room temperature in an airtight container.

SWEET TALK As fresh marshmallows age, the texture will begin to change, with the edges beginning to crystallize, but even then they are great in a cup of coffee or a recipe. They also can be refrigerated or frozen for a couple of months to extend their life, provided they are well protected from air. If stored this way, I recommend wrapping them twice in plastic wrap and then double-bagging them. If they get sticky, just roll them in a little powdered sugar and cornstarch.

BANANA PUDDING ICE CREAM

MAKES ABOUT 1½ QUARTS ★ It's just "nanner puddin'" when it's made with banana pudding mix, a few hits of frozen dairy topping, and some vanilla wafers thrown in for appearance's sake. It's proper banana pudding—and pure grace—when fresh bananas luxuriate in an ice-cold homemade vanilla pudding crowned with a whipped cream or meringue topping. But now this . . . is divine.

2 tablespoons unsalted butter

¼ cup packed light brown sugar

4 ripe bananas, cut into ½-inch slices

2 cups heavy whipping cream

1 cup milk

¾ cup granulated sugar

2 tablespoons cornstarch

2 egg yolks

2 tablespoons banana liqueur or banana flavoring

2 teaspoons vanilla bean paste (see Note) or vanilla extract

1 teaspoon fresh lemon juice

Yellow food coloring (optional, see Note)

2 cups coarsely crumbled vanilla wafers

Garnish: Whole mini or crumbled vanilla wafers, sliced banana

{ continued }

IN a medium skillet, melt the butter over medium heat until bubbly, about 2 minutes. Add the brown sugar and bananas, and stir evenly until the bananas are caramelized and softened, about 2 minutes. Set aside.

IN a large, heavy saucepan, whisk to combine the cream, milk, granulated sugar, and cornstarch over medium-low heat. Cook, stirring constantly, until a candy thermometer reaches 150°F (the mixture will be slightly thickened and coat the back of a spoon), 8 to 10 minutes. Do not let it boil or the mixture will break down. Remove from the heat and set aside.

IN a medium bowl, whisk the egg yolks until slightly thickened. Slowly drizzle in about 1 cup of the warm cream mixture while whisking to incorporate. Pour the cream-yolk mixture back into the saucepan of cream mixture.

WHISK in the liqueur, vanilla bean paste, lemon juice, food coloring (if using), and caramelized banana slices. Use a hand blender to puree the mixture until smooth. Let it rest for about 30 minutes at room temperature before pouring the banana custard into a large container. Cover and refrigerate for 4 hours or overnight.

FREEZE the banana custard in an ice-cream maker according to the manufacturer's instructions. During the last 5 minutes of churning, add the vanilla wafer pieces. Serve immediately, or transfer the banana custard to an airtight container and allow it to harden in the freezer for at least 4 hours. Garnish with wafers or bananas, if desired.

NOTE Vanilla bean paste is an even richer alternative to pure vanilla extract (see Sources, page 200). It can be found at gourmet markets and online. You won't regret the investment—either for this or any other confection. Try mixing a bit of it into some freshly whipped cream and dollop it onto a slice of pie.

Bananas have a way of turning grayish in a pudding or custard, so it's fun to add a few drops of yellow food-color liquid or gel to give it a richer look. I'm just sayin'.

SWEET TALK Homespun ice cream is ideal—and this one is divine—but the Banana Pudding Ice Cream from Texas's Blue Bell Creameries should not be missed under any circumstances. For more on the cult following that Blue Bell enjoys (and why), see page 96.

FROZEN **PEACH CUSTARD**

MAKES 1½ QUARTS ☆ Blushing, cheeky, juicy peaches are Texas's leading fruit crop. By some estimates, there are more than a million trees planted throughout the state. Bushels full of numerous varieties arrive at farmers' markets and supermarkets from late April through the month of July, making the Fourth of July the ideal time to enjoy a sweet peach ice cream under a shady pine or oak tree.

2 pounds fresh unpeeled or frozen sliced peaches (5 to 7 peaches)

1 cup sugar

1 tablespoon light honey (clover, orange blossom)

1 tablespoon fresh lemon juice

1½ tablespoons cornstarch

¼ teaspoon salt

1¾ cups heavy whipping cream

1¾ cups whole milk

4 egg yolks

½ teaspoon vanilla extract

BRING a large pot of water to a boil. In the meantime, prepare an ice bath.

CUT an "X" in bottom of each peach, then blanch them in the boiling water for 15 to 20 seconds to make peeling easier. Use a slotted spoon to transfer each peach to the ice bath to stop the cooking process. Peel the peaches and cut into ½-inch-thick slices.

IN a large bowl, stir the peach slices together with ½ cup of the sugar, the honey, and lemon juice. Refrigerate for at least 8 hours.

IN a medium saucepan, whisk together the cornstarch and salt. Add the cream, milk, and remaining ½ cup sugar and bring just to a boil, stirring until the sugar is dissolved. Remove from the heat.

ADD the egg yolks to a large bowl and add the cream mixture in a slow stream, whisking constantly to temper. (You may need an extra set of hands.) Return the mixture to the saucepan.

COOK the custard over medium-low heat, stirring constantly with a wooden spoon, just until it is slightly thickened and registers 170°F on a thermometer. (Do not let it boil.)

STRAIN through a fine-mesh sieve into a large metal bowl, discarding the solids. Stir in the vanilla. Let the custard cool to room temperature, stirring occasionally. Refrigerate the custard, its surface covered with parchment paper (to prevent a skin from forming), until cold (at least 4 hours).

FREEZE the custard in an ice-cream maker according to the manufacturer's instructions. During the last 5 minutes of churning, add the sliced peaches. Transfer the frozen custard to an airtight container and allow it to harden in the freezer for at least 4 hours before serving.

SWEET TALK If there are eggs in your ice cream, that qualifies it as a custard, which has a denser, creamier texture than traditional ice cream.

MARGARITA SNOW CONES

SERVES 8 TO 10 ★ We Texans love good "margys" (as we're wont to call margaritas). And on a hot-as-blue-blazes day, there's nothing better than an icy one. So I suggest this: If kids can have snow-cone parties, why can't we? Get several squeeze bottles and fill them with your favorite margarita cocktail (mine's below). Buy or borrow a shaved-ice machine and crank up that puppy. Make it the center of attention at a festive beverage play station outfitted with snow-cone cups, squirt bottles of margaritas, plates with lime-flavored salt for cup rimming, pretty bottles of fruit syrups (think Meyer lemon or key lime) fitted with pour spouts, and bowls of varying tropical fruits for added flair and flavor.

2 cups high-quality tequila, preferably agave blanco or reposado

1½ cups fresh lime juice

1 cup orange-flavored liqueur

Shaved ice

Garnish: Fruit syrups, sea salt mixed with lime zest, slices of tropical fruit

COMBINE the tequila, lime juice, and liqueur (in batches) in a cocktail shaker and shake well. Pour into two 24-ounce or three 12-ounce squeeze bottles. Shake well before pouring into snow-cone cups filled with shaved ice. Garnish as you see fit.

SWEET TALK "You can go to hell—I'm going to Texas!"–U.S. Senator and frontiersman Davy Crockett

Dallas's Famous Margarita Machines

Dallas plays a key role in the success of the margarita. Many believe that the insanely popular tequila cocktail (which Americans reportedly drink 185,000 of *every hour*) was concocted by wealthy Dallas socialite Margaret "Margarita" Sames while vacationing in Acapulco in the 1930s. Another Dallasite can officially claim the creation of the very first frozen margarita machine. Back in 1971, restaurateur Mariano Martinez was frustrated by the time it took to whip up one frozen margarita after another. The solution came to him thanks to another Dallas connection: 7-Eleven and its popular Slurpee machine. Martinez tinkered with an old soft-serve ice-cream machine and, well, a star was born. That star permanently resides in the Museum of American History in the Big D.C. (And Mariano's is still going strong in the Big D.)

THE **SWEETEST** TEA

MAKES 2½ QUARTS ★ Throughout Texas, receiving a big cup o' iced tea is as sweet as gettin' an oil royalty check. I learned this from two happy sisters who, thanks to their mama's smart planning, wound up getting those "Texas Tea" checks many years after struggling to survive. Let's just say they don't work 'cause they have to; they work 'cause they want to. One, Barbara Woodley, with her Jiffy-Pop hair and saucer-size eyeshades, is the grand dame of waitresses at Mama's

Daughter's Diner in Dallas, where on occasion she works alongside her equally colorful sister, Natalie Woodley (who also commands star billing at the nearby Original Market Diner). Both sashay around, often with pitchers of tea, having the last word with adorably snarky remarks and donning personality-plus getups. "Life's short," Barbara once advised. "Give it all you got." The same should go for tea. Don't deny yourself the good stuff. Here's the standard way to make it.

10 cups water

2 family-size or 8 regular black tea bags

¾ cup sugar

Garnish: Fresh mint leaves (optional)

BOIL 3 cups of the water, then add the tea bags; continue boiling for 1 minute. Cover and set aside to steep for about 15 minutes.

REMOVE and discard the tea bags. Add the sugar, stirring to dissolve.

POUR the tea mixture into a 1-gallon container, then add the remaining 7 cups water. Stir to combine. Refrigerate until chilled. Serve garnished with a mint leaf. Store in the refrigerator for up to 1 week.

SWEET TALK Keep fruit or herbed syrups on hand to add even more bling to your tea's flavor.

HEAD FOR THE HILLS (OF CENTRAL TEXAS)

Other than the Big Bend area out west, and a few nature preserves along the southern coast, the Hill Country takes the cake for jaw-dropping beauty. It spans the central part of the state though Round Rock, Austin, New Braunfels, Marble Falls, San Saba, Kerrville, Dripping Springs, Llano, Gruene (pronounced "Green"), and even a place named Utopia. At the heart of it all is Fredericksburg, practically a movie set for its Old West–meets-German heritage. This is the realm of limestone and corrugated tin, alt-country music and Willie Nelson, the world's largest Whole Foods and avid nature enthusiasts, the Oasis—where you can watch one of the most glorious sunsets over Lake Austin—and bluebonnets, Shiner Bock, hipster boots, and dance halls.

KERBEY LANE'S **GINGERBREAD** PANCAKES

MAKES 16 PANCAKES ★ Austinites love their breakfasts and brunches, and accordingly, creative options abound—especially at one of the most beloved diner chains in the city, Kerbey Lane Cafe. These treats are just too wonderful for words, so let's hush up and eat.

2 eggs

¼ cup packed light brown sugar

½ cup buttermilk

½ cup brewed coffee (regular or decaf), cold or at room temperature

¼ cup vegetable oil or melted unsalted butter

2 cups all-purpose flour

3 teaspoons baking powder

2 teaspoons baking soda

2 teaspoons ground cinnamon

2 teaspoons ground ginger

2 teaspoons ground nutmeg

½ teaspoon ground cloves

½ teaspoon salt

Garnish: Whipped salted butter, maple syrup

IN a medium bowl, whisk together the eggs and sugar. Add the buttermilk, coffee, and ½ cup water. Stir in the vegetable oil.

IN a medium bowl, mix together the flour, baking powder, baking soda, cinnamon, ginger, nutmeg, cloves, and salt.

ADD the dry ingredients to the wet ingredients, stirring until just combined—don't worry if there are a few lumps.

LIGHTLY grease a large sauté pan or griddle with nonstick spray oil. Heat the pan until hot and then spoon out ¼ cup batter per pancake. Cook the pancakes until the tops look dull and a few of the bubbles pop, about 3 minutes. Turn the pancakes over and cook for another minute or so.

SERVE immediately or transfer the cooked pancakes to an ovenproof dish in a warm oven until the entire batch is finished. Serve garnished with butter and syrup.

SWEET TALK For an even greater flavor depth charge, try these with inventive syrups. I'm thinking cozy cranberry-orange or pomegranate would be especially nice during the holidays or winter. A light citrus one would complement them on warmer days.

APRICOT KOLACHES

MAKES ABOUT 36 KOLACHES ☆ Pilgrims devoted to all things warm, pillowy, and sugary regularly make their way to the tiny town of West, midway between Dallas and Austin. There they find the Little Czech Bakery, essentially a glorified refueling station off I-35, which offers an unrivaled assortment of pastries that have developed a cult following for nearly twenty years. Kolaches— sweet, soft, yeasty rolls filled with various pockets of goodness like apricots, prunes, cheese, or sausage—are much like danishes, only a bit less sweet, and with a more tender texture. In Texas, they're also more meaningful because of the region's Czech heritage. Don't be intimidated by this recipe; it may be time-consuming but it's not brain surgery, and it's so worth it. Once you get the hang of it, you'll enjoy experimenting with other flavors.

APRICOT FILLING

12 ounces dried apricots

3 tablespoons unsalted butter, melted

½ teaspoon almond extract

½ cup sugar, or more to taste

DOUGH

1 tablespoon sugar, plus ½ cup

Two 0.25-ounce packages or 1 tablespoon plus 1 teaspoon active dry yeast

½ cup warm water (110° to 115°F)

2 cups milk

½ cup shortening

3 teaspoons salt

2 egg yolks, lightly beaten

6¼ cups bread flour, sifted (see Note)

6 tablespoons (¾ stick) unsalted butter, melted

CRUMB TOPPING (*POSYPKA*)

⅓ cup all-purpose flour

½ cup sugar

2 tablespoons unsalted butter

{ continued }

TO MAKE THE FILLING: In a medium bowl, cover the apricots with boiling water to rehydrate. Cover the bowl and let them sit overnight or at least 6 hours. Drain excess liquid without squeezing the liquid from the plumped-up apricots.

IN a medium saucepan, heat the rehydrated fruit with the butter and almond extract over low heat, adding the sugar. Use a potato masher to soften and blend the cooked fruit. When it is very soft, remove it from the heat and let the filling cool completely. (For a smoother texture, you can puree the filling in a food processor.)

TO MAKE THE DOUGH: In the bowl of a stand mixer, combine the 1 tablespoon sugar, the yeast, and warm water; set aside until yeast starts to bubble, about 5 minutes.

IN a medium saucepan over medium heat, warm the milk until it registers 98° to 105°F on a candy thermometer. Add the shortening, then let it cool slightly (about 5 minutes). Add the salt, egg yolks, and remaining ½ cup sugar and whisk well.

ADD the milk-egg mixture to the yeast mixture and stir to combine. Add the bread flour, 1 cup at a time, and work with a dough hook or wooden spoon until it is a soft, moist, glossy dough (about the time it begins pulling away from the sides of the bowl).

COVER the bowl with a tea towel, and let the dough rise in a warm, draft-free area until doubled in size, about 45 minutes to 1 hour (for a dough-proofing tip, see Note, page 117).

AFTER the dough has risen, punch it down to remove any air in the dough. Lightly flour a work surface.

USE a tablespoon to remove small portions of dough and drop them onto the floured surface, rolling them into egg-size pieces using the palms of your hands. Place them on greased baking pans in rows of four across and five down (about 1 inch apart) for a pan of twenty. Brush the dough balls with the melted butter. Place them back in a warm, draft-free area, covered with tea towels, to let rise for 20 minutes more.

PREHEAT the oven to 375°F.

TO MAKE THE TOPPING: Combine the all-purpose flour, sugar, and butter in a food processor and pulse until crumbly. (The topping can be made ahead and refrigerated until ready for use.)

MAKE a deep, round impression in the center of each ball of dough and fill it with 1 to 2 teaspoons filling. (Be careful not to press through the bottom of the dough, or the filling will ooze out while baking.) Let the kolaches rise again for 45 minutes to 1 hour.

SPRINKLE the kolaches with desired amount of topping. Bake until golden brown, 20 to 30 minutes (see Note). Let them cool completely and place in a zip-top plastic bag, squeezing all the air out of the bag as you close it.

REFRIGERATE the kolaches for up to 1 week. They are best reheated in the microwave (for one or two kolaches, cook them 15 seconds; for more, 25 to 30 seconds).

NOTE Bread flour offers an airier texture than all-purpose.

Use a lighter-colored baking pan to keep kolaches from browning too quickly; check them often to ensure they don't do just that.

SWEET TALK To save on time, fill kolaches with premade fruit preserves—the chunkier the better. Fig preserves are a personal favorite. Baked kolaches can be frozen for about 2 months, wrapped in plastic and stored in plastic zip-top freezer bags with as much air removed as possible (a straw helps you do just that).

MIGHTY FINE PEACH COBBLER

MAKES ONE 9-×-13-INCH COBBLER ★ Think of the richest, juiciest, fullest flavored, most seductive peaches you can imagine. Then make your way to the Texas Hill Country, where peach growers will surprise you with even more delicious ones than that. The Texas Peach Commission attributes this to the soil loaded with peach-loving micronutrients and minerals. Eating these peaches should be on your "bucket list" if you don't have access to them. This recipe will do you right in the meantime. Just know that I think a good dough is equally important to having fine peaches; that's why I like to make more of it than usual (and everybody loves it when I do just that). If you gobble this up right out of the oven, you needn't worry about the dough absorbing a lot of the liquid. However, once the dessert is stored in the refrigerator, before reheating it, I melt ½ cup (1 stick) butter with ¼ cup or more peach syrup and pour this mixture over the cold cobbler to add a little more liquid.

½ cup (1 stick) unsalted butter

2 cups all-purpose flour

1 cup granulated sugar, plus more if needed

2 tablespoons baking powder

¼ teaspoon salt

2 tablespoons light honey (clover or orange blossom)

1 cup milk

1 tablespoon vanilla extract

5 cups fresh peach slices (about 3½ pounds)

3 tablespoons packed light brown sugar

1 tablespoon fresh lemon juice

1 tablespoon fresh lime juice

½ teaspoon ground cinnamon

¼ teaspoon ground ginger or nutmeg (optional)

Vanilla ice cream or fresh whipped cream for serving

{ continued }

PREHEAT the oven to 375°F. Melt the butter in a 9-×-13-inch baking dish.

IN a medium bowl, combine the flour, ½ cup of the granulated sugar, the baking powder, and salt; add the honey, milk, and vanilla, stirring just until the dry ingredients are moistened. Pour the batter over the melted butter (do not stir).

IN a large, nonreactive saucepan, bring the remaining ½ cup granulated sugar (add more if you like it extra sweet), the peach slices, brown sugar, lemon juice, and lime juice to a boil, stirring constantly, then remove from the heat. Pour the peach mixture over the batter but do not stir. Sprinkle with the cinnamon and the ginger, if desired.

BAKE for about 40 minutes or until golden brown, shielding the crust with foil during the last 10 minutes of baking so that it doesn't overbrown. Serve the cobbler warm with vanilla ice cream or fresh whipped cream. It's also good served cool. It's just plain good. Keep covered in the refrigerator for up to 1 week.

SWEET TALK Stonewall, near Fredericksburg, is home to the Peach Jamboree the third weekend in June. There's even a Peach Trail, where, from Fredericksburg, you can drive east on Highway 290 'til you reach Gellerman Lane. By turning left, you're turning into the sweetest spot in Texas for peaches—about 300 acres of them. Peach stands are in ample supply during the summer months and orchard visits make memorable day trips.

THREADGILL'S PECAN PIE

MAKES ONE 10-INCH PIE ★ Eddie Wilson is the man behind the success that is Threadgill's. His passion for preserving Texas music and home cooking is infectious. And boy does he have stories to tell. He was one of the founders of the infamous Armadillo World Headquarters, a music venue that hosted so many greats—from the up-and-comer-from–Port Arthur Janis Joplin to the already-great Jerry Lee Lewis. Eddie's proud to have taken over the legacy that renegade Kenneth Threadgill started in 1933 when the former bootlegger operated a gas-station-turned-beer-joint. What a long strange trip it's been. And when the time comes to refuel, this pie—his mother Beulah's recipe—will fill your spirit. It's considered one of the best in Texas.

BEULAH'S PIECRUST

1¾ cups all-purpose flour

2 tablespoons granulated sugar

¾ teaspoon salt

6 tablespoons (¾ stick) cold unsalted butter, cut into small pieces

¼ cup cold shortening, cut into small pieces

7 to 8 tablespoons ice water

FILLING

1½ cups packed light brown sugar

5 eggs, lightly beaten

¼ cup (½ stick) unsalted butter, melted

2½ tablespoons all-purpose flour

1⅓ cups light corn syrup

¼ cup dark molasses

1½ teaspoons vanilla extract

2½ cups pecan pieces

Vanilla ice cream for serving (not optional, folks)

{ continued }

TO MAKE THE CRUST: In a large bowl, sift to combine the flour, granulated sugar, and salt. Add the butter and shortening. Use your hands to rub together the ingredients until the fat reaches a pea-size consistency. Add the water and blend until a dough forms. Pat the dough into a ball. Cover and refrigerate for at least 1 hour.

ON a lightly floured surface, roll out the dough to an 11-inch circle. Gently fit it into a 10-inch pie pan and decoratively flute the edges. Refrigerate the unbaked piecrust until needed.

PREHEAT the oven to 350°F.

TO MAKE THE FILLING: Combine the brown sugar, eggs, butter, and flour in a bowl and whisk together. Add the syrup, molasses, and vanilla. Whisk until smooth.

ADD the pecan pieces to the piecrust and pour the filling over the nuts. (They will rise to the top while the pie is baking.)

BAKE for 50 to 60 minutes, or until the filling is completely set in the center (see Sweet Talk). Let the pie cool on a rack for about 1 hour. Slice and serve with a scoop of vanilla ice cream.

STORE leftover pie at room temperature for a day or two. If covered with foil or plastic wrap; it can be refrigerated and kept a couple of days longer. A cooked whole pie can be frozen for a couple of months covered in an airtight container; let thaw in the refrigerator before reheating.

SWEET TALK "If at least one person in ten doesn't think the pie is scorched, it's not done enough to set the crispy sweetness of the pecans and brown sugar." —Eddie Wilson

BUD'S ROUND TOP BUTTERMILK PIE

MAKES ONE 10-INCH PIE ★ This is quintessential Texas: simple and soulful. The recipe for this dense custard pie came off the back of an old Austin Superior Milk Dairy half-gallon container. Now it feeds the masses that pilgrimage to Royers Round Top Café in central Texas, where the Texas flag waves proudly above the old building. Inside, owner/pie master Bud Royer holds forth like a turquoise-laden king. Surrounding him are pies that glisten like edible gems (even the crust looks like prongs holding a diamond ring). The place is always hopping, but especially during the Round Top antique fair held twice a year.

½ cup (1 stick) unsalted butter, at room temperature

3 cups sugar

3 eggs

¼ cup all-purpose flour

1 cup buttermilk

1 tablespoon vanilla extract

¾ teaspoon ground nutmeg

One 10-inch unbaked pie shell or pastry (see page 168)

PREHEAT the oven to 300°F.

IN the bowl of a stand mixer fitted with the paddle attachment, beat together the butter and sugar on medium speed until fluffy. Add the eggs and flour and stir on low until well blended. Add the buttermilk, vanilla, and nutmeg and combine well. Pour into the unbaked pie shell.

BAKE for 1½ hours, or until a toothpick inserted in the center comes out clean. Let cool completely on a wire rack before serving. Cover and refrigerate any leftovers.

SWEET TALK Buttermilk pie is often called "the poor man's pie" because it's so inexpensive to make but has a lovely rich flavor. People often think it's interchangeable with chess pie, but there is a very slight difference between the two: Chess pie has a small amount of cornmeal or corn syrup, which helps give a more gelatinous consistency. Sometimes people call egg custard "buttermilk pie," but the difference there is the addition of scalded milk, not buttermilk.

BUMBLEBERRY CUTIE PIES

MAKES 6 CUTIE PIES OR ONE 10-INCH PIE ★ One of Austin's most endearing people is Jaynie Buckingham, a.k.a. "The Pie Queen." She made her mark in a little pink trailer on South Congress Avenue before moving into a larger space north of town. "I just want this place to trigger memories of happier times," she says. No worries, there. The pie case is an instant magnet.

FILLING

2 cups fresh or thawed frozen blueberries

2 cups fresh or thawed frozen raspberries

2 cups fresh or thawed frozen blackberries

2 cups fresh hulled sliced or thawed frozen strawberries

1 cup fresh or thawed frozen pitted cherries

¼ cup packed light brown sugar

1 tablespoon fresh lime juice

BETTY LOU'S CRUMB TOPPING

1 cup packed light brown sugar

½ cup old-fashioned rolled oats

5 tablespoons all-purpose flour

2 tablespoons cold unsalted butter

Six 4-inch prepared piecrusts
(page 168)

PREHEAT the oven to 350°F.

TO MAKE THE FILLING: In a large bowl, carefully combine the blueberries, raspberries, blackberries, strawberries, and cherries with the brown sugar and lime juice. (A set of clean hands will work nicely for this.)

TO MAKE THE TOPPING: In a medium bowl, mix together the sugar, oats, flour, and butter until the mixture is well blended and crumbly.

SPOON the filling into the crusts and top with the crumb topping.

BAKE for about 15 minutes, or until bubbling. Let the pie(s) cool for a couple of hours before serving. Store loosely covered in the refrigerator for several days.

TEXAS BIG HAIRS
(LEMON-LIME MERINGUE TARTS)

MAKES 8 TARTS ★ Oh, Rebecca Rather, what on Earth would we do without your baking prowess? It's a privilege to feature your lovable Texas Big Hairs here and in your honor, dear "Pastry Queen," we vow to eat these tarts with 'tudes and big smiles on our faces.

TART CRUSTS

1 cup (2 sticks) unsalted butter, at room temperature

1 cup powdered sugar

2 teaspoons vanilla extract

1½ cups all-purpose flour

¼ teaspoon salt

1½ cups coarsely chopped pecans or sliced almonds, toasted (see page 30)

LEMON-LIME CURD

10 egg yolks (reserve whites for meringue)

1½ cups granulated sugar

½ cup fresh lime juice

½ cup fresh lemon juice

Zest of 2 lemons

2 tablespoons unsalted butter

MERINGUE

10 egg whites, at room temperature

3 cups granulated sugar

{ continued }

TO MAKE THE CRUSTS: Grease eight 1-cup 4-inch tart pans.

IN the bowl of a stand mixer fitted with the paddle attachment, cream the butter and powdered sugar on medium-high speed for 3 minutes, until fluffy. Add the vanilla, then gradually add the flour and salt and combine on low speed until incorporated. Add the nuts and mix on low speed until incorporated. Form the dough into a ball (it will be sticky) and cover with plastic wrap. Refrigerate for at least 30 minutes.

PREHEAT the oven to 350°F.

DIVIDE the dough into eight equal portions. Press each one into a prepared pan, making sure it comes up to the top edge of the pan. (Dust your hands with flour periodically to keep the dough from sticking.)

BAKE the crusts about 20 minutes, or until golden brown. Remove and let cool for at least 30 minutes. (Don't worry if the tart bottoms look wrinkly.) At this point, the crusts can be cooled and stored in airtight containers for up to 2 days.

TO MAKE THE CURD: Whisk together the egg yolks, granulated sugar, lime juice, lemon juice, and lemon zest in the top of a double boiler over medium heat. Add the butter and whisk until melted and smooth. Cook for about 40 minutes, stirring lightly with a whisk about every 15 minutes, until the curd is thick, resembling the consistency of loose custard.

TRANSFER the warm mixture to a bowl and cover with plastic wrap, pressing the wrap onto the surface of the curd, sealing it to prevent a skin from forming. Refrigerate for at least 4 hours and up to 3 days. (For express cooling, freeze for least 1 hour.)

TO MAKE THE MERINGUE: Set a large, perfectly clean metal bowl over of a pot of simmering water. (If there is a trace of fat in the bowl, the eggs won't reach their proper volume.) Pour in the egg whites and granulated sugar. Heat while whisking constantly, until the sugar melts and there are no visible grains in the meringue, 5 to 7 minutes. Take a little meringue mixture and rub it between your fingers to ensure all the sugar grains have melted. Remove the bowl from the simmering water and whip the meringue with a mixer fitted with the whisk attachment on low speed for 5 minutes. Increase the speed to high and beat 5 minutes longer, until the meringue is stiff and shiny.

POSITION an oven rack in the center of the oven and preheat the broiler.

SPOON chilled lemon-lime curd into the crusts, filling them about three-quarters of the way to the top. Pile the meringue on top of the curd. Style the meringue with your fingers by plucking at it to tease into jagged spikes. (Having a bit of meringue stuck to your fingers will help you form big spikes.)

SET the tarts on the middle rack of the oven and broil until the meringue topping turns golden brown, about 1 minute. Watch the tarts closely, as they can burn in a matter of seconds. (If using a kitchen torch, hold it 2 to 3 inches away from the meringue and move the flame slowly around the meringue until is browned all over.) The tarts should be eaten the day they are assembled.

SWEET TALK If you can't get to Rebecca's Rather Sweet Bakery, tucked back off the main drag in Fredericksburg, you can at least get to try some of her good works in a couple of books that are mandatory for dessert lovers—*Pastry Queen Parties*, *The Pastry Queen Christmas*, and the book that started it all: *The Pastry Queen* (from whence this recipe originates).

YES, **SAUERKRAUT CAKE**

MAKES ONE 8-INCH DOUBLE-LAYER CAKE ★ I know what you're thinking. But you're wrong, my friend. For nearly a century this cake has been made in the New Braunfels area of Texas, where my friend Dale Dietert's mother has made it, and her mother made it, and so on and so forth all the way back to the old country (Germany). This is like a German chocolate cake, 'cept with 'kraut, which not only comes across as coconut but also keeps the cake moist.

CAKE

²⁄₃ cup well-rinsed and drained sauerkraut

²⁄₃ cup unsalted butter, at room temperature

1¹⁄₃ cups granulated sugar

3 eggs

1 teaspoon vanilla extract

2¹⁄₄ cups all-purpose flour, sifted

¹⁄₂ cup unsweetened cocoa powder

1 teaspoon baking powder

³⁄₄ teaspoon baking soda

¹⁄₄ teaspoon salt

1¹⁄₄ cups brewed coffee or water, at room temperature

ICING ON THE CAKE

¹⁄₂ cup (1 stick) unsalted butter, at room temperature

8 ounces cream cheese, at room temperature

3 cups powdered sugar

¹⁄₄ cup unsweetened cocoa powder

1 teaspoon vanilla extract

TO MAKE THE CAKE: Preheat the oven to 350°F and grease and flour two 8-inch round or square baking pans. Set aside.

PULSE the sauerkraut in a food processor a few times to ensure a super-fine consistency. Pat dry with paper towels to absorb excess brine (it is essential to remove as much briny flavor as possible). Set aside.

IN a stand mixer fitted with the paddle attachment, beat together the butter and granulated sugar until creamy. Beat in the eggs and vanilla.

IN a medium bowl, combine the flour, cocoa powder, baking powder, baking soda, and salt, and add them to the butter mixture alternately with the coffee. Mix just until combined. Stir in the sauerkraut. Pour the batter into the prepared pans.

BAKE for 30 minutes, or until a toothpick inserted in the center of a cake comes out clean. Let the cakes cool in the pans for 15 minutes, then invert them onto racks to cool completely.

TO MAKE THE ICING: In a stand mixer fitted with the paddle attachment, cream together the butter and cream cheese until well blended. Add the powdered sugar, cocoa powder, and vanilla and stir to combine well.

SPREAD the icing evenly between the cooled layers and over the top and sides of the cake. Store the cake at room temperature beneath a cake cover if planning to eat within a day, or refrigerate, tented with plastic wrap, for up to 3 days. Let the cake return to room temperature (this takes about 1 hour) before serving.

SWEET TALK This is one of those "surprise" desserts that has a secret ingredient no one will guess. For other such recipes, see pages 90 and 142.

GERMAN CHOCOLATE CARROT CAKE

MAKES ONE 10-INCH CAKE ★ Arlene Lightsey is one of Texas's most respected cooks and restaurateurs. Foodies still pine for her Old Post Office Café in Comfort, near New Braunfels. I know I do. (And so do hordes of others; the café's related spiral-bound cookbook from 1991 may be out of print, but it has a cult following, selling for at least $50 if you can find one.) This cleverly simple recipe represents why. Two yummy cakes combined as one? It's a real "twofer."

CAKE

3 cups all-purpose flour

2 cups granulated sugar

2 ounces German sweet chocolate, grated

2 teaspoons ground cinnamon

1½ teaspoons baking soda

1½ teaspoons salt

1 teaspoon baking powder

1½ cups vegetable oil

One 8-ounce can crushed pineapple, drained

3 eggs

2 teaspoons vanilla extract

2 cups peeled, grated raw carrots

1½ cups finely chopped walnuts

1¼ cup currants or raisins (optional)

NUTTY CREAM CHEESE FROSTING

2½ cups powdered sugar

4 ounces cream cheese, at room temperature

3 tablespoons butter, at room temperature

1 tablespoon vanilla extract

1 to 2 tablespoons milk

¼ cup chopped walnuts

¼ cup currants or raisins (optional)

TO MAKE THE CAKE: Preheat the oven to 350°F and grease and flour a 10-×-3½-inch Bundt pan.

IN the bowl of a stand mixer, combine the flour, granulated sugar, chocolate, cinnamon, baking soda, salt, and baking powder. Mix on low to blend.

ADD the vegetable oil, pineapple, eggs, and vanilla. Beat on medium speed for 3 to 4 minutes, until well combined.

FOLD in the carrots, walnuts, and currants (if using) by hand. Pour into the prepared pan.

BAKE for 75 to 90 minutes, or until a toothpick inserted in the center comes out clean.

COOL in the pan for 10 minutes before removing the cake from the pan and letting it cool completely on a wire rack.

TO MAKE THE FROSTING: In the bowl of a stand mixer with the paddle attachment, combine the powdered sugar, cream cheese, butter, vanilla, and milk. Mix on medium speed until smooth and creamy. Stir in the walnuts and currants (if using) by hand.

FROST the cooled cake with the cream cheese frosting. Store the cake at room temperature beneath a cake cover if planning to eat within a day, or refrigerate, tented with plastic wrap, for up to 3 days. Let the cake return to room temperature (this takes about 1 hour) before serving.

1886 CHOCOLATE CAKE

MAKES ONE 9-×-13-INCH CAKE ★ Austin's posh spice comes from the Driskill Hotel, a Western-style four-story mansion of limestone and the oldest operating inn in the city. Upon its completion in 1886 by cattle baron Col. Jesse Driskill, it was called "the finest hotel south of St. Louis." The place still retains its swank factor, and this dense rich chocolate cake, which reportedly has been served there since the beginning, has something to do with that. Note that it is similar to the Good Ol' Texas Sheet Cake (page 177) but has more cocoa and buttermilk, and a refined silky glaze for more richness all around. And it is delicious topped with vanilla ice cream and fresh raspberries.

CAKE

2 cups cake flour

2 cups granulated sugar

1 teaspoon baking soda

1 cup buttermilk

2 eggs, lightly beaten

2 teaspoons vanilla extract

1 cup (2 sticks) unsalted butter

½ cup unsweetened cocoa powder

CHOCOLATE GLAZE

½ cup (1 stick) unsalted butter

½ cup unsweetened cocoa powder

1 teaspoon vanilla extract

2 cups powdered sugar

¼ cup buttermilk or more, for desired spreadability

1 cup chopped pecans, toasted (see page 30; optional)

{ continued }

TO MAKE THE CAKE: Preheat the oven to 350°F and grease a 9-×-13-inch baking pan. Set aside.

IN a large bowl, combine the flour, granulated sugar, and baking soda.

IN a medium bowl, stir to combine the buttermilk, eggs, and vanilla.

IN the top of a double boiler, combine the butter, cocoa powder, and ⅔ cup water and heat until the butter is melted; stir to combine.

ADD the butter mixture and egg mixture to the flour mixture. Stir by hand until well mixed.

POUR the batter into the prepared pan.

BAKE for 40 to 45 minutes, or until a toothpick inserted in the center of the cake comes out clean. Cool in the pan while preparing the glaze.

TO MAKE THE GLAZE: In a medium, heavy-bottomed saucepan over medium heat, melt the butter, and stir in the cocoa powder and vanilla until well blended; add the powdered sugar. Whisk to combine and add the buttermilk until it has a smooth, pourable consistency.

RELEASE the cake from the pan onto a cake plate. Pour the warm glaze over the cake, allowing the cake to soak it up. Top with the pecans, if desired. Cut into 2½-inch squares and serve.

STORE the cake at room temperature beneath a cake cover if planning to eat within a day, or in the refrigerator, tented with plastic wrap, for up to 3 days. Let the cake return to room temperature (this takes about 1 hour) before serving.

VERY BERRY TRIFLE IN A JAR

SERVES 8 ★ Despite my grandmother, "Aunt Freddie" Bailey, being a real pro at canning (selling her jellies and preserves to such fans as Bob Hope and Lucille Ball), I didn't inherit that gene. I did, however, inherit a lot of the glass jars she collected, and over the years I've added to them, coveting many of the ones found while antiquing. My fascination with them and love of their myriad patterns has evolved from using them as vases and vessels for summer drinks to showcasing layered salads in them and, now, layered desserts. These are so much fun to serve at picnics. And use any mix of fruit you'd like. And, if time's short, use a ready-made pound cake.

LEMON POUND CAKE

1½ cups all-purpose flour

1 teaspoon baking powder

½ teaspoon salt

1 cup (2 sticks) unsalted butter, at room temperature

1½ cups sugar

4 eggs, at room temperature

2 teaspoons vanilla extract

¼ cup fresh lemon juice

1 tablespoon lemon zest

FILLING

¾ cup heavy whipping cream

½ cup sugar

8 ounces cream cheese, at room temperature

1 teaspoon vanilla extract

1 teaspoon fresh lemon juice

1 teaspoon lemon zest

1 cup fresh blueberries

1 cup fresh raspberries (mix of yellow and red, if available)

{ continued }

TO MAKE THE CAKE: Preheat the oven to 350°F. Butter an 8½-×-4½-inch loaf pan and line it with parchment or wax paper.

IN a medium bowl, stir to combine the flour, baking powder, and salt.

IN a stand mixer fitted with the paddle attachment, beat the butter at medium speed until creamy. Add the sugar and mix until fluffy. With the mixer running at low speed, add the eggs, one at a time, then the vanilla.

ADD the dry ingredients to the butter mixture alternately with the lemon juice and zest, beginning and ending with the flour. Mix after each addition until just blended.

POUR the batter into the prepared pan and bake for 65 to 75 minutes, or until raised in the center and a toothpick inserted into the center comes out clean.

LET the cake cool in the pan for 15 minutes (it will still be warm). Run a knife around the sides of the pan. Turn the cake out onto a wire rack. Peel off the paper.

TO MAKE THE FILLING: In a medium bowl, beat the cream with ¼ cup of the sugar until stiff peaks form.

IN another bowl, stir to combine the cream cheese, vanilla, lemon juice, lemon zest, and remaining ¼ cup sugar. Fold the whipped cream into the cream cheese mixture.

IN a medium bowl, crumble the pound cake, ensuring that the crumbles remain chunky and not too fine.

LINE the bottom of eight medium (16-ounce) widemouthed canning jars with about 1 inch of cake pieces, followed by 2 tablespoons blueberries, then some cream mixture, then 2 tablespoons raspberries, then another layer of cake, then more cream mixture. Top with a final layer of berries (and maybe a sprinkling of lemon zest) and cover and refrigerate until serving.

SWEET TALK I love Bonne Maman jams, and I especially love the vintage-style jars, with their red-and-white-checked caps, that they come in. Tie a ribbon round 'em, add a fun label, and you've got instant food gifts. If you can't find them in a local supermarket, see Sources on page 200.

ANCHO-CHOCO TRUFFLES

MAKES 24 TRUFFLES ☆ This recipe hails from one of my favorite chile experts, the late great Jean Andrews, a brilliant, eccentric Austinite who called these babies "New World Truffles" in her book *Red Hot Peppers*. Ten years ago, the mainstream appreciation for chiles had just stemmed; it indeed was a New World Order in the culinary landscape. "I was into peppers before being into peppers was so hot," she once told me, adding that she came from "a long line of Southern women known for their cooking skills." These ancho chile–graced truffles are sweet with just a hint of smokiness. "I've always believed in taking the dull edge off," Jean said. And that she did.

1½ cups milk chocolate chips

¼ cup (½ stick) unsalted butter

1 tablespoon ground ancho chile powder (see Note)

½ teaspoon cayenne pepper

½ cup egg substitute (see Note)

2 tablespoons Kahlúa liqueur or brandy

1 cup finely ground pecans

PUT the chocolate chips and butter in the top of a double boiler set over barely simmering water. Cover and allow them to warm for 1 or 2 minutes, or until partially melted. Remove the lid and stir together until well combined.

REMOVE the double boiler with the chocolate mixture from the heat (keeping the water simmering) and add the ancho and cayenne to the mixture; stir well. Stir in the egg substitute and set over the simmering water. Stir the mixture until hot but not boiling, about 3 minutes.

REMOVE the mixture from the heat and gradually stir in the liqueur. Set the pan in a large bowl of ice water, adding ice as needed to keep the surrounding water very cold. Stir constantly until the mixture forms a fairly firm, nonsticky ball.

{ continued }

PLACE rounded teaspoonfuls of the candy on a baking sheet lined with wax paper. Cover loosely with plastic wrap and allow the candy to sit at room temperature until firm enough to handle (1 to 2 hours).

PUT the pecans on a sheet of wax paper and roll each ball of candy in the nuts to form evenly coated truffles. Let the truffles sit at room temperature for another 30 minutes to 1 hour and shake off any loose nuts.

REFRIGERATE until very cold and then serve. Store in an airtight container for up to 1 week in the refrigerator.

NOTE Ancho chile powder, made from dried poblano peppers, can be found in the Latino food section of most large supermarkets, at Latino food marts, or by ordering online (for a source, see page 200).

Jean used an egg substitute as a food safety precaution, since this recipe is cooked at a low temperature.

Since these truffles are a tad soft, its best to store them in the refrigerator and serve them very cold.

ALMOND FLAN À LA FONDA SAN MIGUEL

MAKES ONE 9-INCH FLAN ★ Austin's premier authentic Mexican hacienda-style restaurant, Fonda San Miguel, transports you to interior Mexico. The colorful traditional décor, with its contemporary Mexican art and handmade furnishings, is a work of art. So is this silky, sweet flan, with a texture akin to cool sliceable velvet infused with almonds. The acclaimed chef for the place simply known as "La Fonda," Miguel Ravago, is just as smooth and sweet.

¾ cup sugar

2 cups sweetened condensed milk

1 cup whole milk

⅔ cup blanched, slivered almonds

3 eggs

3 egg yolks

1 teaspoon vanilla extract

Garnish: Orchid and mint sprigs or toasted almond slivers and whipped cream (optional)

PREHEAT the oven to 350°F and place an oven rack in the middle position.

PUT the sugar in a round 9-inch cake pan. Use tongs to place the pan directly over medium heat to caramelize the sugar. Heat until the sugar liquefies, 3 to 5 minutes, stirring occasionally with a wooden spoon. (Do not touch the melted sugar; it will cause serious burns.)

WHEN the hot liquid sugar in the pan is golden brown, remove the pan from the heat to a rack to cool and harden.

IN a blender or food processor, combine the condensed milk, whole milk, almonds, eggs, egg yolks, and vanilla. Process on medium speed until well blended. Pour the custard mixture over the prepared caramel in the baking pan. Place the cake pan in a larger, deeper pan and pour about 1 inch of hot water around the cake pan to make a water bath. Cover the flan loosely with a foil tent and place the larger pan on the middle rack of the preheated oven.

BAKE for 1 hour and 15 minutes, or until the flan is set in the center. Remove from the oven and water bath and cool the flan in the pan on a rack at room temperature. Refrigerate until thoroughly chilled, at least 1 hour.

RUN a knife or thin spatula around the edge of the flan to release it from the sides of the pan. Place a 10-inch or larger serving platter on top of the pan. Turn the platter and cake pan over and gently remove the cake pan, leaving the flan on the serving platter. Using a flexible spatula, scrape up as much of the caramel as possible from the bottom of the pan and pour it over the flan. Garnish, if desired. Cut into triangular wedges and serve. Cover and refrigerate any leftovers for up to 1 week.

The Beauty of Blue Bell

After tasting for the first time the inventive flavors of this exceptional custard-like ice cream—perhaps the Banana, Peaches & Homemade Vanilla, Southern Blackberry Cobbler, Birthday Cake, or Strawberry Cheesecake flavors—one newbie's reaction, as stated on an ice-cream forum was this: "Oh. My. God."

'Nuff said. We Texans are pretty proud of Blue Bell Creameries.

Based in Brenham, the creamery got started in 1907 after local farmers decided to make butter from excess cream. A few years later, the Brenham Creamery Company began making ice cream and delivering it to neighbors by horse and wagon. And by 1930, the company changed its name to Blue Bell Creameries to honor the native Texas bluebell wildflower.

At the time of this book's printing, Blue Bell was only available in about 26 percent of the nation's supermarkets, but it ranks as one of the top three best-selling ice creams in the country. The company's products are sold primarily in the South and Southwest but also in Indiana, Kansas, and Ohio. For those interested in visiting the ice-cream mecca, its production facility offers tours. And for those who just want to eat it and can't buy it locally, never fear—it can be ordered.

CHOCOLATE I SCREAM SANDWICHES

MAKES ABOUT 22 SANDWICHES ✦ Scream with happiness, that is. Since it's just plain hot in Texas, ice-cream sandwiches are just as common as ice in freezers. But store-bought ones can taste— let's face it—store-bought. They can be so much fun to make, though, especially with kids, or for one of their parties. Here's a recipe for the classic "sandwich" cookie that you can create and, using an ice chipper or pick or the tines of a fork, create the iconic little holes that give the cookies a classic look. You can roll the sides of ice-cream sandwiches in chopped nuts, tiny chocolate chips, crushed peppermints, or candies. And dip them in melted white, milk, or dark chocolate.

2¾ cups all-purpose flour, plus more for dusting

½ cup unsweetened cocoa powder

2½ teaspoons baking powder

¼ teaspoon salt

¾ cup (1½ sticks) unsalted butter, at room temperature

2 cups sugar

2 tablespoons vanilla extract

2 eggs

2 tablespoons milk

2 to 2½ pints of your favorite ice cream

IN a medium bowl, sift together the flour, cocoa powder, baking powder, and salt; set aside.

IN a stand mixer fitted with the paddle attachment, cream together the butter, sugar, and vanilla until fluffy.

ADD the eggs and milk to the butter mixture, and mix until just combined. Add the flour mixture, and mix on low speed until incorporated, about 2 minutes, scraping down the sides of the bowl with a spatula at least once.

DIVIDE the dough in half, and shape each half into a roughly flat disk. Wrap each disk in plastic wrap, and refrigerate until firm, about 1 hour. (They will keep refrigerated for about 1 week.)

PREHEAT the oven to 350°F.

{ continued }

ROLL out one disk of the dough on a lightly floured surface to ¼ inch thick. Working quickly to ensure the dough stays cold, use a knife, or a 3-inch biscuit or cookie cutter, and cut out about 22 cookies. Make sure there is an even number, to provide a top and bottom cookie for each sandwich. Put them on baking sheets lined with parchment. Use an ice chipper or fork tines to prick holes all over the surface of the cookies, if desired. Repeat with the other disk of dough, if desired, or save it for another time.

BAKE for 12 to 14 minutes, until just firm. Let the cookies cool slightly on the baking sheet, then transfer them to a wire rack to cool completely.

REMOVE the ice cream from the freezer to let it soften slightly, 10 to 12 minutes. Spread the ice cream about ½ to 1 inch thick in between each set of cookies. Wrap each ice-cream sandwich in freezer wrap. Transfer them immediately to the freezer to harden, at least 1 hour.

SERVE directly from the freezer and let thaw slightly before eating. The sandwiches can be stored in an airtight container in the freezer for about 1 week.

Freeze Frames

Here's a way to create some quickie ice-cream sandwiches with store-bought cookies and Blue Bell ice cream.

★ Chocolate chip cookies with Happy Tracks ice cream (vanilla, chocolate-coated peanut butter cups, and dark fudge)

★ Shortbread cookies with Pecan Praline ice cream

★ Lemon cookies with Strawberry ice cream

★ Oatmeal cookies with Pistachio Almond or Spiced Pumpkin Pecan ice creams

★ Graham crackers with Caramel Turtle Fudge ice cream

★ Snickerdoodles with Coffee ice cream

★ Sugar cookies with Rocky Road ice cream

★ Peanut butter cookies with Banana Split ice cream

★ Chocolate cookies with Peppermint ice cream

★ Gingerbread with Orange Swirl ice cream

★ Poundcake slices with Peaches & Homemade Vanilla ice cream

★ Waffles with Cherry Cheesecake ice cream

★ Madeleines with Chocolate-Covered Strawberries ice cream

BIG RED GRANITA

MAKES ABOUT 3 QUARTS ★ Nothing's better than an ice-cold sody pop, unless it's a frozen one. Take, for instance, this one. Big Red—one of the most popular soft drinks in Central and South Texas—made its debut in Waco back in 1937. At first it was called Sun Tang Cola, but since it's really just a red cream soda, it morphed into Sun Tang Big Red Cream Soda until "Big Red" stuck in the 1960s. It boasts a big ol' burst of bubblegum-like flavor, with hints of orange, lemon, and vanilla.

GRANITA

2 liters Big Red or strawberry soda

MINT SYRUP (OPTIONAL)

1 cup sugar

1 cup water

12 to 14 fresh mint leaves

Garnish: Mint sprigs (optional)

TO MAKE THE GRANITA: Pour the soda into a 4-quart or two smaller freezer containers. Cover tightly and freeze until solid, at least 4 hours.

TO MAKE THE SYRUP (IF USING): In a medium saucepan, combine the sugar and water and heat to a boil while stirring. Reduce the heat and continue to stir while the sugar dissolves. Add the mint leaves. Set aside and let cool.

POUR the syrup through a fine-mesh strainer fitted into a funnel inserted into a sealable container and refrigerate for up to a couple of months.

USE an ice pick or knife blade to break apart the frozen soda into flaky crystals.

SPOON the granita into cups. For a refreshing twist, pour about 1 teaspoon mint syrup on top and garnish if desired. Tightly covered, this will keep in the freezer for about 1 month.

SWEET TALK Big Red can leave some big red stains on your clothing if you're not careful, so be a sweetheart and keep lots of napkins and some stain remover on hand while guests are shoveling this down (which they will be prone to do with abandon).

SOUTH TO THE BORDER

The South Texas plains and coastal region, spanning from Del Rio in the west to San Antonio on over to Corpus Christi in the east, down to Harlingen and Brownsville and on over to Laredo, encompasses a unique confluence of Mexican-American and Anglo-American traditions, architecture, and food. By proximity, the Rio Grande Valley is heavy on Mexican influence, which contributes mightily to the state's beauty and flavor. This is the land of the Alamo in San Antone, the King Ranch in Kingsville (825,000 acres geared to raising cattle and horses), Native American tribes, the lower Gulf of Mexico, and pristine bird-watching refuges. And color—lots of it. With vibrant people to match.

LUCKY BUÑUELOS
WITH HONEYED FRUIT SALSA

MAKES ABOUT 24 BUÑUELOS ★ Like the Deep South tradition of cooking black-eyed peas and cabbage for good luck at the start of the New Year, the Tex-Mex version is the making of buñuelos. Eating them is thought to bring families good luck, and the beauty is often that the entire family participates in making them. Sometimes they're made as fried dough balls (and are more like little doughnuts), but they're often served as fried disks or as little triangles. And in many cases they're drenched in a super-sweet fruit sauce or a passel of honey. I prefer the triangular fashion, thinking of them almost like sweet tortilla chips and eaten like nachos. And as for that sauce, a light fruit salsa brings them more up to date. If time's short, just fry fresh flour tortillas for a similar effect.

HONEYED FRUIT SALSA

1 cup diced fresh mango

1 cup diced fresh kiwi

1 cup diced fresh pineapple

¼ cup light honey

¼ cup chopped pecans or pine nuts, toasted (see Note, page 30; optional)

2 tablespoons chopped fresh mint

2 tablespoons fresh lime juice

BUÑUELOS

3 cups all-purpose flour

1 tablespoon baking powder

1 teaspoon salt

½ cup (1 stick) unsalted butter, melted

2 eggs

1 teaspoon vanilla extract

1 tablespoon sugar plus ½ cup

¾ cup milk, plus more if needed

1 teaspoon ground cinnamon

½ teaspoon ground ginger

Vegetable oil, for frying

TO MAKE THE SALSA: In a medium bowl, mix the fruit, honey, pecans (if using), mint, and lime juice together. Refrigerate for at least 30 minutes to let the flavors unite.

TO MAKE THE BUÑUELOS: In a large bowl, sift together the flour, baking powder, and salt.

IN a medium bowl, beat the butter, eggs, vanilla, and 1 tablespoon sugar. Add the milk and stir to combine. Add the egg-milk mixture to the flour mixture and stir to make a dough, adding more milk, ¼ teaspoon at a time, if the mixture is too dry.

KNEAD the dough on a lightly floured surface until smooth and roll it out to ¼ inch thick. Use a pizza cutter to cut it into triangles, squares, or rectangles, or use small cookie cutters to make stars. Cover with a tea towel and let stand for 30 minutes.

IN a small bowl, combine the remaining ½ cup sugar, the cinnamon, and ginger.

IN a large, deep skillet, heat about 2 inches of oil to 360°F.

FRY the dough in batches until golden brown, turning once. Drain on paper towels and sprinkle with the cinnamon-ginger sugar.

PUT about six buñuelos in a dish and top with ⅓ to ½ cup fruit salsa to serve.

SWEET TALK Make extra fruit salsa and enjoy it over grilled pork, fish, or shrimp. Or cheesecake. Definitely cheesecake. Tightly covered, the salsa will keep for about 3 days in the fridge.

CHURROS BUENOS

MAKES ABOUT 24 CHURROS ★ These deep-fried pastries are like thin doughnuts rolled in cinnamon and sugar. And they're highly addictive. Churros have been a Texas tradition for centuries, having been favored by Spanish *vaqueros*—the earliest cowboys, who drove cattle from the Texas plains to Mexico City—for the ease of frying them over a campfire.

2½ tablespoons sugar, plus ½ cup

2 tablespoons vegetable oil, plus more for frying

½ teaspoon salt

1 cup all-purpose flour

3 eggs

1 teaspoon ground cinnamon

IN a small saucepan over medium heat, whisk to combine 1 cup water with the 2½ tablespoons sugar, vegetable oil, and salt. Bring to a boil and remove from the heat. Stir in the flour until the mixture forms a ball.

REMOVE the dough to large bowl. Let it cool to room temperature for 3 minutes (the mixture will be very hot). Add the eggs, one at a time, using a hand mixer to blend them in after each addition.

POUR the vegetable oil to a depth of 3 inches into a deep fryer or skillet and heat to 365°F.

USE a cookie press with the large star disk or a pastry bag fitted with a large star tip to pipe 3- to 4-inch strips of dough into the hot oil. (You can also use a use zip-top plastic bag with a corner clipped off, but the strips will be more globular.)

FRY the churros in batches of four or five until golden, 2 to 3 minutes; drain them on paper towels. (The dough strips will gravitate to one another, but use a slotted spoon to keep them separated or gently pull them apart later.)

COMBINE the remaining ½ cup sugar and the cinnamon. Roll the drained churros in the cinnamon-sugar mixture and serve them warm.

SWEET TALK *Churro* means "fritter" in Spanish. They are often served with hot chocolate.

SWEET PINEAPPLE TAMALES
WITH COINTREAU CREAM

MAKES 16 TO 18 TAMALES ☆ Tamales are the original "wrap"—introduced to Texas by way of Central America and Mexico. They're so commonplace here, and so inexpensive, that many of you might wonder why on earth you'd take the time to make your own. But once you've actually enjoyed, or been a part of the making of, homemade tamales you do understand what all the fuss is about. Dessert versions are made mostly for celebrations—Christmas, New Year's, Day of the Dead, weddings, birthdays, anniversaries—where lots of people can enjoy them. The pineapple (*piña*) version is a perennial favorite, but here it's dressed up for the occasion with bow ties (corn husks) and Cointreau Cream.

TAMALES

20 to 24 corn husks

2 cups diced fresh pineapple

2 tablespoons packed light brown sugar, plus ¼ cup

½ teaspoon orange zest

¾ teaspoon ground cinnamon

2¼ cups premade masa (see Note)

1 teaspoon baking powder

¼ teaspoon salt

1¼ cups fresh orange juice

½ cup shortening

COINTREAU CREAM

1 cup heavy whipping cream

¼ cup powdered sugar

1½ tablespoons Cointreau liqueur

Garnish: Orange zest (optional)

TO MAKE THE TAMALES: Tear 6-inch-long strips from 3 or 4 corn husks to make 16 to 18 ties. Put the corn husks and strips into a large bowl of warm water. Weigh them down with a smaller bowl of water filled with pie weights or water. Set aside to soak for 30 minutes.

IN a medium bowl, combine the pineapple, 2 tablespoons brown sugar, orange zest, and ¼ teaspoon of the cinnamon. Set aside.

IN another medium bowl, combine the masa with the remaining ¼ cup brown sugar, remaining ½ teaspoon cinnamon, baking powder, and salt. Add the orange juice and ¾ cup water and stir until a soft dough forms.

IN the bowl of a stand mixer fitted with the paddle attachment, beat the shortening on medium speed until fluffy. Add the masa mixture and beat to combine.

DRAIN and pat dry the corn husks, then lay them out in a single layer. Spread about 2 tablespoons of the masa mixture over the center of each open corn husk. Top with several of the cinnamon-sugar pineapple pieces (about 1 tablespoon). Wrap each husk tightly around the filling and fold in the ends; tie each tamale with a corn husk strip. Cover and refrigerate until ready to steam.

TO MAKE THE CREAM: In a chilled medium metal bowl, whip the cream (with cold beaters) on high for 3 to 4 minutes, until stiff peaks form. Add the powdered sugar and whip on low until just blended; repeat with the Cointreau. Refrigerate until ready to use.

PREPARE a covered steamer basket over boiling water. Steam the tamales in a single layer for about 55 minutes, until warm through. Allow them to cool slightly.

UNWRAP and serve each tamale with a dollop of Cointreau Cream. Garnish, if desired.

NOTE Premade masa is best purchased from a tortilla factory or Latino grocery store. If fresh premade masa isn't available, used dried masa harina and follow the directions on how to reconstitute it.

SWEET TALK Other sweet tamale ideas to consider: strawberry, rhubarb, blueberry, raspberry, peach, apple, date, pumpkin, banana, chocolate . . . yum. Add cream cheese to the filling for even more indulgence.

Wrapped in Family Tradition: Tamaladas

Throughout Texas, especially South Texas, the latter part of fall is a steamy affair. That's when celebratory tamale-making sessions (*tamaladas*) are in full gear—beginning around *Día de Los Muertos* (November 1, when ancestors are lovingly and festively paid tribute) and running through *Las Posadas* (December 16 to 24, representing the biblical journey of Joseph and Mary to find safe shelter in a foreign land—a story holding special significance for Mexican immigrants) and on through Christmas and into the New Year. This is when it doesn't cost a bundle to give a bundle—of love and flavor.

The tamale-filling menu might include spicy pork, chicken and green chile, black bean and corn, plus something sweet for dessert. Then the *tamalada* marathon unfurls in whichever house is selected. (They often rotate from house to house to help create new sets of memories, especially for younger family members.)

Everyone gets a task. Some chop, someone makes the masa, others stuff, some wrap the tamales with banana leaves or corn husks, others oversee the steaming process and cleaning along the way. *Chisme* (friendly family gossip) is told all the while, fueled by camaraderie that's encouraged by sweet punch, kicky sangria, and ice-cold beer.

Stacks of metal stands—many that are handmade, passed down through the generations—go into big pots. These days, tamale pots with steamer inserts are easy and inexpensive to buy (for resource information, see page 200). Makeshift ways of steaming them include stacking collapsible steamer baskets in a large stew pot or using a pasta steamer insert; some place a stack of metal pie plates with holes punched in them, turned upside down in the middle of the pot, and begin to lay in the tamales on a slant that way. More creative sorts even use nesting Chinese dim-sum steamers, with bigger versions available from restaurant supply companies or online. In all cases, the racks

holding the tamales should be at least 2 inches away from gently boiling water underneath.

What's made on Christmas Eve day, for instance, is typically savored after midnight mass that evening, helping to kick-start the festive day ahead.

Culturally, the making of the tamales signifies fellowship, yes, but also abundance and fulfillment—two things families definitely want the New Year to bring.

I've always cherished the *tamalada* tradition for this reason: You don't have to reinvent the "wow" factor that goes into crafting a Thanksgiving dinner. It takes a load of pressure off. And since the premade masa at Latino supermarkets or gourmet supermarkets is often quite good, that shaves even more time off the cooking process. Or, you can simply buy the tamales from restaurants. But make sure you get your order in early: popular places like San Antonio's Delicious Tamales are in high gear this time of year.

One fulfilling aspect is being able to buy them from churches and other charitable organizations, which host their own *tamaladas* to raise money to continue doing their good works.

PAN DULCE CONCHAS

MAKES 12 ROLLS ★ So many *panaderías* (bakeries), so little time. Each one has its own subtle ways of presenting traditional Latin American breads, often in well-worn metal trays in wooden rolling racks or glass-front cases. It's sensory overload with all the aromas, but the most eye-catching of the lot are the dome-shaped sweet rolls topped with colored sugar. The ones I love the most have the nautilus shell–inspired *concha* carvings atop them. *Just how do they do that?* I've often marveled. It was high time to find out. Here's just one way it's done, but like family *mole*, each recipe—some denser, others more light and fluffy—is unique and honed over time. Here's one that's a little of both. It's a bit time-consuming to get the hang of, but once you figure out which end is up, you can start perfecting your own favorite.

CONCHAS

3 teaspoons active dry yeast

½ cup very warm water

½ cup evaporated milk

½ cup powdered sugar

¼ cup (½ stick) plus 2 tablespoons unsalted butter, melted but not hot

2 eggs, at room temperature, lightly beaten

1 teaspoon salt

3½ cups all-purpose flour, sifted

½ teaspoon ground cinnamon

SUGAR TOPPING

1 cup all-purpose flour

½ cup powdered sugar

½ cup granulated sugar

½ cup shortening

3 teaspoons vanilla or almond extract

Pink and yellow (or other desired colors) gel food colors (optional)

Garnish: Sugar or cinnamon-sugar (optional)

{ continued }

TO MAKE THE CONCHAS: In the bowl of a stand mixer, combine the yeast and warm water. Stir and let sit for 10 minutes or until foamy.

IN a small saucepan, heat the evaporated milk until just warm (less than 1 minute over medium heat) or microwave for 20 seconds.

IN a stand mixer with the paddle attachment, combine the yeast mixture with the milk, powdered sugar, butter, eggs, salt, and 1¾ cups of the flour. Mix for 2 to 3 minutes, then gradually mix in the remaining 1¾ cups flour, and add the cinnamon.

WHEN the dough begins pulling away from the sides of the bowl, put it onto a floured counter to knead for 8 to 10 minutes, or until smooth and elastic.

PLACE the dough in a large greased bowl, and turn the dough to coat. Cover with a tea towel, and let rise in a warm place until doubled in size, from 1 hour to 1½ hours (see Note).

TO MAKE THE TOPPING: After letting the dough rise for 40 minutes, mix the flour, both sugars, shortening, and vanilla in a food processor until the mixture is a smooth, paste-like consistency. (If it appears too dry, add a little milk to make it more pliable.)

DIVIDE the topping into three parts and place each in a separate bowl, one for each color topping—white (uncolored), pink, and yellow (or other colors as desired)—and mix in the food colors. Divide each bowl of topping into four balls, and pat them flat on a lightly floured surface.

WHEN the dough is done rising, cut it into twelve even pieces. Shape them into 3-inch-wide domed balls, and place them on two greased or parchment-lined baking sheets (six on each), about 3 inches apart.

DIP a pastry brush in a small amount of warm water and brush the tops of the dough balls.

PRESS each portion of the topping between your palms until flat. Place each portion on one dough ball. Pat it slightly so that it conforms to the dough's round top.

USE a knife to gently cut grooves in the topping like the swirls of a nautilus shell. (You also can carve grooves in a crisscross pattern.) Cover with tea towels and let rise until nearly doubled, 45 minutes to 1 hour.

PREHEAT the oven to 375°F.

BAKE the conchas for 15 to 18 minutes, or until lightly golden brown. Let them cool slightly before garnishing with sugar, if desired.

NOTE: To ensure you have a warm place (we Texans usually have lots of warm places in our homes), here's a trick: An hour before making this recipe, turn the oven to 200°F and place a small heat-proof dish of water on the bottom rack of the oven. Once preheated, turn off the oven, leaving the bowl of water in place. Put the dough in the warm oven to rise.

Higher altitudes need less rising time, so the dough may double in bulk faster. Keep an eye on it. Also, you may need less flour; if so, try ½ cup less if the mixture turns out drier than you'd like.

SWEET TALK This is just one of the many pastries that originated during France's rule of Mexico, in the early 1860s, when Mexico was brimming with traditional French bakeries. Ever since, Mexicans have loved crisp baguettes and rich sweet breads. (Though the French themselves, not so much: Cinco de Mayo celebrates Mexico's independence from France on May 5, 1862.)

MEXICAN WEDDING COOKIES

MAKES ABOUT 24 COOKIES ★ At best, these are powdered baked clouds that melt marvelously on the tongue. At worst they're—well, OK, so they're never at their worst. I'm more Tex-Mex than Mex-Mex when it comes to making these, opting more for the "Mexican wedding cookie" look (frosted) rather than what my friends of Mexican descent simply refer to as *pan de polvo*, or *polvorones*, adding a bit of anise and eschewing that follow-up roll in powdered sugar (which I like to do twice).

1 cup (2 sticks) unsalted butter, at room temperature

1½ cups powdered sugar

1 teaspoon vanilla extract

¼ teaspoon salt

1¾ cups all-purpose flour

1 teaspoon ground cinnamon

1 cup ground toasted pecans, walnuts, or almonds (see page 30)

IN a medium bowl, use a hand mixer on high to whip the butter until light and fluffy. Add ½ cup of the powdered sugar and whip on high until light and fluffy again. Add the vanilla and salt and, with the hand mixer on low, combine until just blended.

IN a medium bowl or on a sheet of wax paper, sift together the flour and cinnamon. Add to the butter mixture. Add the nuts and stir with a wooden spoon or spatula until blended. Cover and refrigerate for at least 1 hour.

PREHEAT the oven to 350°F.

SHAPE the dough into 2-inch balls. (A small cookie scoop comes in handy for this.) Place them about 1 inch apart on an ungreased cookie sheet and bake for 15 to 18 minutes, or until the cookies are just golden on the bottom. Remove them to cool on wire racks for about 5 minutes.

IN a medium bowl or on a sheet of wax paper, sift the remaining 1 cup powdered sugar. Roll the warm cookies in the sugar and return them to the racks to cool. Once the cookies are cool, roll them again. Store at room temperature in an airtight container for about 1 week.

SWEET TALK These are served less at weddings and more at Christmastime. They make great gifts. My grandmother used to add 1 tablespoon bourbon or rum to the batter.

PUMPKIN EMPANADAS

MAKES ABOUT 12 EMPANADAS ★ Empanadas are Latino turnovers and gobbled up in savory and sweet versions. The sweet ones endear themselves to me for so many reasons, but especially for the variety of fillings they often harbor. This one's yummy in fall, especially when served with vanilla bean ice cream and sprinkled with a bit of nutmeg. Or maybe topped with chocolate or dulce de leche sauce or . . .

EMPANADA DOUGH

2 cups all-purpose flour

1/2 teaspoon salt

1/2 teaspoon ground cinnamon

2/3 cup shortening

FILLING

One 15-ounce can pure pumpkin

1/2 cup sugar

1/2 teaspoon ground cinnamon

1/4 teaspoon ground ginger

1/4 teaspoon salt

2 eggs (optional)

Sugar for sprinkling (optional)

TO MAKE THE DOUGH: In a large bowl, combine the flour, salt, and cinnamon. Add the shortening and use a hand mixer to combine. Add 1/3 cup water and mix to thoroughly combine.

KNEAD the dough in the bowl to incorporate any remaining flour. Divide the dough into four dough balls and wrap each one in plastic wrap. Refrigerate for about 1 hour (or up to 2 days in an airtight container).

TO MAKE THE FILLING: In a medium bowl, combine the pumpkin, sugar, cinnamon, ginger, and salt and stir well to combine. Set aside.

PREHEAT the oven to 350°F.

DIVIDE each dough portion into four equal parts. Slap the dough balls between well-floured hands until slightly flattened, and then roll them out on a lightly floured surface to about 4 inches wide and about 1/8 inch thick.

SPOON about 1 tablespoon of filling into the center of each circle. Fold over, pressing the edges to seal them in a wavy edging or press with fork tines. Place them on parchment-lined baking sheets 1 inch apart.

{ continued }

MAKE an egg wash, if desired, by whisking the eggs with 2 tablespoons water in a small bowl.

BRUSH each empanada with egg wash (if using) and sprinkle with more sugar, if desired.

BAKE for about 20 minutes, until golden brown. (Watch them closely; they can burn fast.) Remove the empanadas to wire racks to cool slightly. Serve warm or let cool completely and refrigerate, well wrapped, for up to 2 days.

NOTE: Frozen empanadas can be reheated in a 350°F oven for 25 minutes.

SWEET TALK In a pinch, try Goya's empanada turnover puff pastry disks, "Tapas para Empanadas," available in the frozen-food section at Latino food markets. I keep a pack of twelve in the fridge for serving with fruit fillings when the mood strikes. Another tip: Don't get too filling-happy, or your turnovers will runneth over.

LUBY'S CHOCOLATE **ICEBOX PIE**

MAKES ONE 9-INCH PIE ★ Texans hold a special place in their hearts for Luby's, which opened in 1947 in San Antonio and spread like gossip after church. The cafeteria has been a Sunday dinner mainstay for millions of families. Part of the Luby's allure is its dessert offerings, with this icebox pie often being one of them. Icebox pie has long been a favorite in the sizzling Lone Star State 'cause you don't have to heat up the kitchen to make it. And you gotta open the face-cooling icebox to fetch it.

PIE

2½ cups milk

2 cups (4 sticks) unsalted butter or margarine

1⅓ cups sugar

¼ cup unsweetened cocoa powder

7 tablespoons cornstarch

3 egg yolks

1 teaspoon vanilla extract

1 cup miniature marshmallows

One 9-inch prebaked pie shell (see page 168)

SWEETENED WHIPPED CREAM

1 cup heavy whipping cream

¼ cup sugar, or more to taste

½ teaspoon vanilla extract

Garnish: Chocolate curls or shavings (see Note)

TO MAKE THE PIE: In a medium saucepan, combine 2 cups of the milk, the butter, sugar, and cocoa powder. Bring to a boil over medium heat.

IN a medium bowl, mix the cornstarch with 6 tablespoons water until the cornstarch is completely dissolved. Stir in the remaining ½ cup milk. Whisk in the egg yolks and vanilla until well blended.

ADD the cornstarch-egg mixture, gradually, to the milk mixture in the saucepan, stirring constantly with a whisk.

COOK over medium heat, stirring constantly for about 2 minutes, or until the mixture is thickened and smooth. Add the marshmallows and stir until they are melted and the mixture is smooth.

POUR into the pie shell. Press plastic wrap directly onto the filling (to prevent a "skin" from forming while cooling) and refrigerate for at least 2 hours.

TO MAKE THE WHIPPED CREAM: In a chilled metal bowl, whip the cream (with cold beaters) with the sugar and vanilla on high for 2½ to 3½ minutes until soft peaks form; keep refrigerated until ready to use.

REMOVE the plastic wrap from the pie and top the pie with the whipped cream. Garnish if desired. The pie should keep, tented with plastic wrap or foil (or better yet, with a high-dome cover), in the refrigerator for about 4 days.

NOTE To make chocolate curls, use a potato peeler to shave strips from a solid chocolate bar.

SWEET TALK I can't help but smile when watching the animated show *King of the Hill* (now, sadly, in reruns) to see Hank Hill's family dine at "Luly's." The show also features country ingenue Luanne Platter (whose Texas twang was executed brilliantly by the late actress Brittany Murphy). "The Lu Ann Platter" is actually a half entrée with two vegetables and a roll at Luby's.

POTEET STRAWBERRY CAKE

MAKES ONE 8-INCH TRIPLE-LAYER CAKE ☆ Now then, those pink cakes made from cake mixes and gelatin have kitsch and sentimental appeal—I tend to think of them rotating in cake-slice displays in old-school steakhouses, or adding a little bling to a church-social banquet table. But in this case, let's kick it old-school—way old-school—back to the days when fresh was the only game in town. I had a cake similar to this one years ago at one of my favorite Texas celebrations: the Strawberry Festival held each April in Poteet, thirty minutes south of San Antonio. I've spent my days since then trying to re-create that hallowed memory. This comes pretty darn deliciously close.

CAKE

2 cups granulated sugar

1 cup (2 sticks) unsalted butter, at room temperature

2 cups pureed fresh or thawed frozen strawberries

½ cup sour cream

1 teaspoon vanilla extract

1 teaspoon lemon extract

1 teaspoon lemon zest

3 cups cake flour (see Note)

1 tablespoon baking powder

1 teaspoon baking soda

¼ teaspoon salt

5 egg whites

STRAWBERRY CREAM CHEESE FROSTING

1 pound cream cheese, at room temperature

½ cup (1 stick) unsalted butter, at room temperature

6 cups powdered sugar, sifted (or more to taste)

½ cup mashed ripe fresh strawberries, drained well

Garnish: Fresh strawberry slices

{ continued }

TO MAKE THE CAKE: Preheat the oven to 350°F and grease and flour (or coat with baking spray) three 8-inch round cake pans; set aside.

IN the bowl of a stand mixer fitted with the paddle attachment, beat the granulated sugar and butter at medium speed until creamy. Add the pureed strawberries, sour cream, vanilla, lemon extract, and lemon zest.

IN a large bowl, stir to combine the flour, baking powder, baking soda, and salt. Add to the mixer bowl and stir just to combine.

IN a cold and clean metal bowl, use cold beaters to beat the egg whites until stiff peaks form. Gently fold them into the batter.

POUR the batter evenly into the prepared pans, smoothing the tops with an icing spatula to ensure evenness.

BAKE for 22 to 25 minutes, rotating the pans halfway through, until the tops spring back when gently pressed and a toothpick inserted in the center of the cakes comes out clean.

TRANSFER the pans to a wire rack to cool for 10 minutes. Unmold the cakes onto the racks and allow them to cool completely top-side up.

TO MAKE THE FROSTING: In the bowl of a stand mixer fitted with the whisk attachment, combine the cream cheese and butter on low speed for about 30 seconds. Add the powdered sugar and strawberries and blend on low until well incorporated. Increase the speed to medium and mix for an additional minute, until the frosting texture is fluffier.

SPREAD the frosting between the cooled cake layers, then over the top and sides; garnish with sliced strawberries, if desired. Refrigerate the cake for about 30 minutes to set the icing.

STORE the cake, tented with plastic wrap or in an airtight cake container, in the refrigerator for about 1 week or freeze in an airtight container for several months (just thaw in the refrigerator overnight before serving). Keep refrigerated before and after serving.

NOTE: As a substitute for the 3 cups cake flour, place 6 tablespoons cornstarch in a 1-cup measure and fill the rest with all-purpose flour before leveling off and placing in a medium bowl. Then add another 2 cups all-purpose flour to the bowl.

SWEET TALK When I was a little girl, red velvet (see page 34) was my birthday cake of choice. But had I had the pleasure of tasting this one, it would have been my choice. Little ones might enjoy the addition of colored sprinkles, candy buttons, or SweeTarts candies.

THE STRANGE FAMILY'S
CARAMEL-APPLE CAKE

MAKES ONE 9-INCH CAKE ☆ The only thing Strange about this recipe is the name of the man who created it: Don Strange (1940–2009), potentate of the world-renowned San Antonio ranch-based catering company still going strong in South Texas and beyond. (Braggin' rights alert: Strange and his team have hosted barbecues on the White House lawn. And with so many talented 'cue makers in Texas, that's saying something.) This family can cook. And this cake was one of Don's favorites—down-to-earth and not too fussy. Just good. Just right.

CAKE

1½ cups vegetable oil

2 cups granulated sugar

3 eggs

3 cups all-purpose flour

1 teaspoon baking soda

3 cups peeled and diced Granny Smith apples (about 3 large), patted dry

1 cup chopped pecans, toasted (see Note, page 30)

2 teaspoons vanilla extract

CARAMEL GLAZE

1¼ cups packed light brown sugar

¾ cup (1½ sticks) unsalted butter

½ cup evaporated milk

TO MAKE THE CAKE: Preheat the oven to 350°F and grease and flour a 9-×-3-inch Bundt pan. Set aside.

IN a large bowl, whisk together the vegetable oil and granulated sugar, then beat in the eggs, one at a time. Add the flour and baking soda and blend well.

FOLD in the apples, pecans, and vanilla to the batter. (Note: It is very important that the apples be dry; if necessary, dry them further with paper towels.)

POUR the batter into the prepared pan and smooth the top. Bake for 1 hour to 1 hour 20 minutes, or until a toothpick inserted in the center of the cake comes out clean. Cool in the pan at least 10 minutes before inverting onto a wire rack to cool completely.

TO MAKE THE GLAZE: In a small saucepan, mix the brown sugar, butter, and milk. Bring to a boil over medium heat, stirring constantly. Remove from the heat. Let the glaze cool completely (about 30 minutes).

DRIZZLE the cake with the glaze to serve.

THE cake can be stored at room temperature beneath a cake cover if planning to eat within a day, or refrigerated, tented with plastic wrap, for up to 3 days. Let the cake return to room temperature (this takes about 1 hour) before serving.

PUT THE LIME IN THE COCONUT CAKE

MAKES ONE 9-INCH DOUBLE-LAYER CAKE ★ When the Food Network challenged some of the nation's best bakers to crank out some of the nation's top cakes on *Ultimate Recipe Showdown*, the prize for "Best Birthday Cake" went to this exceptional offering by San Antonio's Doreen Haller-Howarth. She really knows how to bake. Her family-run Cakery bakery is a downtown magnet for inventive offerings like this, which happens to be one of my favorite cakes now, too. Happy birthday to me. And to you.

CAKE

1 cup (2 sticks) unsalted butter, at room temperature

2 cups granulated sugar

2 teaspoons coconut oil (see Sources, page 200)

4 eggs, at room temperature

2½ cups all-purpose flour

1 teaspoon baking soda

½ teaspoon baking powder

½ teaspoon salt

1 cup coconut milk

COCONUT GLAZE

1 cup sour cream or plain yogurt

1 cup shredded unsweetened coconut

⅔ cup granulated sugar

Zest and juice (about ⅓ cup) of 2 to 3 limes

¼ cup coconut milk

COCONUT FROSTING

½ cup (1 stick) unsalted butter, at room temperature

½ cup shortening, at room temperature

4 ounces cream cheese, at room temperature

3 cups powdered sugar

¼ cup coconut milk

2 cups shredded unsweetened coconut

TO MAKE THE CAKE: Preheat the oven to 350°F and grease and flour two 9-inch round cake pans.

IN the bowl of a stand mixer fitted with the paddle attachment, cream the butter and granulated sugar on medium speed until fluffy. Add the coconut oil and then the eggs, one at a time, mixing after each addition.

IN a medium bowl or on parchment paper, combine the flour, baking soda, baking powder, and salt. Add the coconut milk and flour mixture to the butter mixture alternately, beginning and ending with the flour mixture.

DIVIDE the batter between the prepared pans. Bake for 25 to 28 minutes, or until a toothpick inserted in the center of a cake comes out clean. Allow to cool in the pans for 10 minutes, then unmold onto wire racks and allow to cool completely.

TO MAKE THE GLAZE: In a medium bowl, combine the sour cream, coconut, granulated sugar, lime zest and juice, and coconut milk.

LAY a long sheet of plastic wrap on the counter. Spoon a thin, 9-inch-round layer of glaze (about one-fourth of the mixture) onto one section of the plastic wrap and place one cake on top of the glaze. Use a bamboo skewer to poke holes in the cake and spread another

one-fourth of the glaze on top of the cake. Wrap in plastic wrap. Repeat the process with the other cake. Refrigerate both glazed cakes until ready to frost, or at least 40 minutes.

TO MAKE THE FROSTING: In the bowl of a stand mixer fitted with the paddle attachment, beat together the butter, shortening, and cream cheese until well blended and fluffy. Add the powdered sugar gradually on low speed and beat in the milk.

REMOVE the cakes from the plastic wrap, using a spatula to scrape any excess glaze onto the cakes. Put one layer on a plate or cake stand and spread with about ½ cup of the frosting. Top with the other layer. Spread the remaining frosting on the top and sides of the cake and press the shredded coconut into the frosting. Store the cake at room temperature beneath a cake cover if planning to eat within a day, or refrigerate, tented with plastic wrap, for up to 3 days. Let the cake return to room temperature (this takes about 1 hour) before serving.

CORA'S HUMMINGBIRD CAKE

MAKES ONE 9-INCH TRIPLE-LAYER CAKE ★ Aunt Cora Bailey reveled in being a Southern lady—and typing in a faint cursive on her little pink typewriter with its own carrying case. *And* sporting fiery red hair in an updo. *And* wearing pearls with everything. But most of all, especially later in life after losing her husband "Cutesy," she loved to bake. Prolifically. This cake reminds me so much of her. She was originally a South Louisiana transplant whose family was from Mobile way. Though she was a *gringa* extraordinaire, I bet she made many a friend with such cakes as this one, which definitely won my family's heart from the earliest of days. Many food historians believe the tropical-fruit cake originated in some fashion in Jamaica, where the hummingbird is the national bird, before making its way north to the South.

HUMMINGBIRD CAKE

3 cups all-purpose flour

2 cups granulated sugar

1 teaspoon baking soda

1 teaspoon ground cinnamon

1 teaspoon salt

1½ cups safflower or vegetable oil

3 eggs, lightly beaten

One 8-ounce can crushed pineapple, undrained

2 cups mashed bananas (3 to 4)

1 cup chopped pecans, toasted (see Note, page 30)

1½ teaspoons vanilla extract

PECAN-CREAM CHEESE FROSTING

1 pound cream cheese, at room temperature

1 cup (2 sticks) unsalted butter, at room temperature

3½ cups powdered sugar, sifted

½ cup finely chopped pecans, lightly toasted (see Note, page 30)

1 tablespoon lemon zest

2 teaspoons vanilla extract

Garnish: Pecan halves, lemon zest (optional)

{ continued }

TO MAKE THE CAKE: Preheat the oven to 350°F and grease three 9-inch round cake pans with butter; dust the bottom and sides with flour. Set aside.

IN a large bowl, combine the flour, granulated sugar, baking soda, cinnamon, and salt and stir until well blended.

ADD the safflower oil and eggs, and stir until the dry ingredients are moistened. Stir in the pineapple and juice, bananas, pecans, and vanilla.

DIVIDE the batter evenly among the prepared pans. Bake for 25 to 30 minutes, until a toothpick inserted into the center of the cakes comes out fairly clean. Let the cakes cool in the pans for about 10 minutes, then remove them to wire racks to cool completely.

TO MAKE THE FROSTING: In a stand mixer fitted with the paddle attachment, beat the cream cheese and butter until fluffy. Gradually add the powdered sugar and whip until smooth. Add the pecans, lemon zest, and vanilla and combine well.

PLACE one cooled cake layer on a serving plate. Spread about ½ cup frosting on top, then cover with another cake layer. Spread another ½ cup frosting on top and cover with the last layer. Spread the remaining frosting over the top and sides of the cake. Garnish by placing pecan halves in a decorative pattern around the cake and sprinkle the top with lemon zest, if desired. Store, covered, in the refrigerator for about 1 week.

SWEET TALK Make additional layers for this cake by doubling the batter and using less per pan to make thinner cakes; that's what Aunt Cora used to do when she wanted it to look pretty. She also put some pansies on top. I thought she named this after some of the hummingbirds she fed 'round her home. Only later, while working at *Southern Living*, did I realize this cake has a cult following—thanks in large part to said magazine, which popularized it.

SEN. ZAFFIRINI'S **PRALINE PECANS**

MAKES ABOUT 6 CUPS ☆ Texas State Senator Judith Zaffirini, a Democrat from the border city of Laredo, is on the winning side of history. The longtime former teacher is the first Latina senator in Texas. She's also very popular: She has, on occasion, carried all seventeen counties in her large and diverse district during re-election, something no one else has ever accomplished.

"This recipe is as easy to prepare as the product is delicious," Senator Zaffirini says. It's particularly meaningful to her because it was given by a friend whose memory she treasures, the late Barbara Kazen of Laredo. "She was a gourmet cook who shared many of her favorite recipes with me," she says. "Every time I make these, I think of her and of the joy and love she brought into so many lives." Senator Zaffirini's son (see him as a boy on page 203) cherishes that his mom makes these for their large extended family every Christmas Eve, serving the praline-coated pecans (alongside twenty other desserts!) and giving them as gifts in heart-shaped boxes.

2 cups sugar

1 cup buttermilk

1 teaspoon baking soda

2 tablespoons unsalted butter

6 cups pecan halves

IN a 6-quart heavy saucepan, stir to combine the sugar, buttermilk, and baking soda over medium-high heat. Bring to soft-ball stage (234 to 240°F) on a candy thermometer, stirring frequently to prevent burning. (As the candy cooks, it will turn golden brown.)

REMOVE from the heat and stir in the butter until melted and combined. Add the pecans and stir to coat all the nuts.

SPREAD the candy on a countertop or baking sheet lined with wax paper; once the candy has cooled enough to be touched, separate any pecans that have clumped together and allow the candied nuts to cool completely. Store in an airtight container for several weeks.

SWEET TALK This recipe works out best on those Texas days with low humidity; otherwise, the candy gets sticky.

ORANGE-KISSED FIG ICE CREAM

MAKES ABOUT 1½ QUARTS ★ Fig trees work their charm throughout Texas, providing much-appreciated shade and, if they hold their own against wily birds, lots of fruit—especially the farther south you go. Maybe because my grandmother made fig preserves with oranges, I love to pair the two flavors. And naturally, with the triple-digit temps usually accompanying their arrival, the idea of citrus-infused fig ice cream—made just as she'd make orange ice cream—is not only a refreshing thought, but a sentimental one as well.

2 pounds fresh ripe figs (about 20), plus more for garnish

2¾ cups fresh orange juice, pulp removed

1½ cups heavy whipping cream

¾ cup sugar

½ cup half-and-half

1 tablespoon orange zest

1 tablespoon fresh lemon juice

1 teaspoon vanilla extract

Garnish: Fresh fig slices, orange zest

STEM the figs, then cut them into small pieces. Put them in a medium, nonreactive saucepan and cover with ¾ cup of the orange juice and ¼ cup water. Cover and cook over medium heat, stirring occasionally, for about 10 minutes, or until the figs are soft. Remove from the heat and let cool uncovered for at least 30 minutes. Drain the figs, reserving the pulp.

IN a large bowl, stir to combine the fig pulp, remaining 2 cups orange juice, the cream, sugar, half-and-half, orange zest, lemon juice, and vanilla. Cover and refrigerate for at least 8 hours or overnight, until the mixture is very cold.

FREEZE the fig mixture in an ice-cream maker according to the manufacturer's instructions. Serve immediately, or pack into freezer containers and freeze until firm. Garnish, if desired.

SWEET TALK Fig trivia: When Spaniards settled in Texas and California, they brought with them fig plants for their missions. That's the age-old variety that's now called the Mission fig.

HATCH CHILE AND AVOCADO ICE CREAM

MAKES ABOUT 1 QUART ★ We eat a lot of chiles in Texas, but never do we get more excited about them than during the late-summer Hatch chile season. That's when the New Mexican beauties make their appearance here, and many devotees scamper immediately to the one place that puts them on a pedestal: Texas's own gourmet chain, Central Market. There the peppers are not only roasted daily (*oh*, how wonderful they are in mac 'n' cheese) but are also showcased in an ever-changing mix of creative recipes cooked up by CM's creative foodies. (They even have an app devoted to the chiles.) There's a recipe contest each year, and a recent winner caught my eye—a recipe developed by food blogger Adele Williams of San Antonio. Chiles and avocados in ice cream? The creamy avocados I can see, but chiles? I just had to try it. And how happy I was to embark on the adventure. The result is an earthy-sweet, only slightly edgy treat in a lovely shade of sage green. I love offering this treat to unsuspecting friends, usually at outdoor cookouts. Washed down with a col' beer, it's just plain delicious. And lots of fun to discuss.

2 large eggs

½ cup sugar, plus 2 teaspoons

¼ teaspoon sea salt

1½ cups whole milk

1 cup light or regular vanilla ice cream

2½ teaspoons vanilla extract

1 to 2 fresh Hatch chiles, finely minced

2 ripe avocados, peeled and mashed

1 tablespoon lime zest (about 1 lime)

1 tablespoon fresh lime juice (about ½ lime)

Garnish: Whipped cream, lemon or lime zest, sea salt (optional)

CRACK the eggs into a medium mixing bowl. Add the ½ cup sugar and whisk until the mixture is frothy and lemon yellow in color. Add ⅛ teaspoon of the sea salt and stir to combine.

IN a medium saucepan over medium heat, heat the milk until it just begins to simmer, then remove from the heat. Slowly add the warm milk to the egg mixture, a little at a time, whisking constantly, until all the milk has been added.

POUR the egg-milk mixture back into the pan and cook over medium-low heat, whisking constantly until the mixture thickens (about 7 minutes). Remove from the heat and strain into a bowl. Let cool slightly (about 5 minutes). Stir in the ice cream and 2 teaspoons vanilla. Refrigerate until very cold (at least several hours).

IN a large bowl set into an ice bath (to keep the ingredients cold), combine the chiles, avocados, lime zest, lime juice, and the remaining ½ teaspoon vanilla, 2 teaspoons sugar, and ⅛ teaspoon sea salt. Stir in the ice-cream mixture and mix well. Freeze in an ice-cream maker according to the manufacturer's directions. Serve garnished with a dollop of whipped cream and sprinkled with lemon or lime zest and sea salt, if desired. This will keep well in the freezer in an airtight container for a couple of days.

SWEET TALK Adele likes to serve this green goddess in a wine, martini, or margarita glass.

Central Market: Central to Good Eating

In 1905, Florence Butt opened the C.C. Butt Grocery Store in Kerrville, northwest of San Antonio, with an investment of $60. I'd say that's a fine investment. Her youngest son, Howard E. Butt, took over the family business in the 1920s, the brand of markets eventually became known by Howard's initials, H-E-B. Today, H-E-B–now headed by Howard's youngest son, Charles Butt–is Texas's largest private company (with 330 and counting supermarkets) and the number-one retailer in South and Central Texas.

H-E-B's crowning jewel is its upscale "amusement park for food lovers" that, like its competitor Whole Foods, got its start in Austin. Charles Butt's concept of a European-style fresh market got its start in 1992, and twenty years later H-E-B draws an average of two million visitors each year. Other Central Market stores have opened in San Antonio, Houston, Dallas, Plano, Fort Worth, and Southlake. And I speak for all Texas foodies when I say it truly is one of my main reasons for living.

MINTY MELON POPS

MAKES 16 POPSICLES ★ Whenever you have melon, you rarely have just a little. You have lots of it. This is a great way to use that leftover melon. Think of it as *agua fresca* on a stick. (And you know how we love our sticks o' anything.)

MINT-LIME SYRUP

1 cup sugar

1 cup water

¼ cup loosely packed fresh mint

½ cup fresh lime juice

POPSICLES

1 cup pureed watermelon (black seeds removed)

1 cup pureed honeydew melon

1 cup pureed cantaloupe

TO MAKE THE SYRUP: Combine the sugar and water in a medium saucepan and heat to a boil, stirring constantly until the sugar dissolves. Add the mint and set aside; let cool to room temperature. Pour the mint syrup through a strainer into a clean container, add the lime juice, and stir to combine. Refrigerate for up to 2 weeks.

TO MAKE THE POPSICLES: Using three medium bowls, keep the pureed melons separate.

POUR equal amounts of mint-lime syrup into each melon bowl and stir well.

FILL popsicle molds three-fourths full (leaving room for expansion) with individual melon mixes or a combination of them (see Note). Set the lids in place and insert sticks through the holes. If you don't have popsicle molds, fill small freezer-proof cups about three-fourths full; stretch plastic wrap across the top and affix with rubber bands. Make ½-inch slits in the center and insert sticks.

FREEZE the popsicles until firmly set (3 to 4 hours).

REMOVE the popsicles by squeezing the sides of the molds or cups and twist slightly to disengage. If necessary, briefly rinse the outside of the molds or cups under hot water.

NOTE: For a layered, rainbow effect, freeze each mold, fitted with a stick, about one-third full and keep frozen for about 1 hour or more before adding the second layer of a different juice. Let it freeze for about 1 hour more before adding a third layer of a different juice, then freeze until completely firm.

WHERE THE WILD WEST MEETS THE MILD PLAINS

This vast, rugged section of our fine state is the one I'm certain most people around the world picture when they think of Texas. From the Panhandle's Amarillo down to Lubbock on over through Abilene and to Fort Worth, and from El Paso down to Big Bend Country (with Marfa and Alpine), all the Texas stereotypes are here: arid cactus-studded deserts, windswept plains, rodeos, cowboys, canyons, big shiny belt buckles, pickups, tumbleweed, and horses. Think of it as the lower Midwest morphing into New Mexico, with an edginess that comes out in its music (Bob Wills, Buddy Holly, Lyle Lovett, Robert Earl Keen). Yup. Keep it simple, but keep it good.

HOMEMADE FUNNEL CAKES
WITH SPIKED WHIPPED CREAM

MAKES ABOUT 8 FUNNEL CAKES ★ Native son Jon Bonnell (of Bonnell's Fine Texas Cuisine), is one of Fort Worth's most beloved chefs. And fathers. And friends. Here's one of the reasons for all of the above: a recipe suited to both lil' kids and big kids. "Fried sweet dough dusted with liberal amounts of cinnamon-powdered sugar is a pleasure to be sure," Jon says. Besides that, "this recipe will turn any ordinary parent into an immortal hero at a kid's party." Funnel cakes are indulgent, he admits, but honestly now, who doesn't love one—especially at the State Fair? Made at home, "they're worthy of the effort down to each finger-licking bite," says Jon.

SUGAR-CINNAMON DUST
(NOT OPTIONAL)

½ cup powdered sugar

1 tablespoon ground cinnamon, or more to taste

SPIKED WHIPPED CREAM
(OPTIONAL)

2 cups heavy whipping cream

1 teaspoon powdered sugar

1 teaspoon light brown sugar

3 tablespoons bourbon

¼ teaspoon ground cinnamon

FUNNEL CAKES

2 cups all-purpose flour

1 tablespoon granulated sugar

1 teaspoon baking powder

1 teaspoon salt

1½ cups milk

2 eggs

⅔ teaspoon vanilla extract

⅓ cup butter, melted

Vegetable oil, for frying

{ continued }

TO MAKE THE SUGAR-CINNAMON DUST: In a zip-top plastic bag, shake to combine the powdered sugar and cinnamon. Pour it into a flour sifter to sift onto the funnel cakes when ready to serve.

TO MAKE THE WHIPPED CREAM: In a chilled metal bowl, whip the cream (with cold beaters) until soft peaks form.

DISSOLVE both sugars in the bourbon and add to the whipped cream along with the cinnamon. Whip until medium peaks form. Set aside and keep refrigerated until ready to serve.

TO MAKE THE FUNNEL CAKES: In a medium bowl, sift together the flour, granulated sugar, baking powder, and salt.

IN a stand mixer fitted with the whisk attachment, blend the milk, eggs, and vanilla. Slowly add the flour mixture and whisk just until the mixture becomes light and fluffy. Drizzle in the butter and mix until combined.

POUR the batter into a pastry bag with a round tip or a plastic bag with a corner cut out of it. (In either case, crimp the tip or corner of the bag upward so the batter doesn't run out before it needs to.)

IN an electric fryer or deep heavy pot, pour vegetable oil to a depth of at least 3 inches and heat to 360°F. (This is where electric fryers earn their keep for keeping the temperature even; you don't want that oil to get any lower than 350°F, or you'll get soggy funnel cakes.)

PIPE the cake batter into the hot oil in a crisscross pattern. Fry for 1 minute on each side, or until golden brown. Drain the funnel cakes on paper towels. Top with Sugar-Cinnamon Dust and Spiked Whipped Cream, if desired, and serve.

SWEET TALK "I think Texans have more fun than the rest of the world." —Legendary choreographer/dancer/singer Tommy Tune, born in Wichita Falls

SPICY CHOCOLATE-PEPITA COOKIES

MAKES FORTY-EIGHT 4-INCH COOKIES ☆ Some 460 miles west of the Bush ranch, and a world away in artsy mindset, is Marfa—home not only to Katherine Shaughnessy and her grandmother's lemon cake (see page 180), but also to the Food Shark, one of the coolest food trucks on the planet. Overseen by chef Krista Steinhauer and her husband and chief driver, Adam Bork, the silver rolling eatery—a 1974 delivery truck—dishes out Arabic/Mediterranean cooking, West Texas–style (i.e., the "Marfalafel"). It's accompanied by a converted dine-in school bus for bad-weather days. For nibbles, here's a cookie that's as quirky as its venue.

1 cup old-fashioned rolled oats

2 cups all-purpose flour

1½ tablespoons dark cocoa powder (see Sources, page 200)

1 teaspoon salt

1 teaspoon baking soda

1 teaspoon baking powder

¼ teaspoon ground cinnamon

⅛ teaspoon ground cloves

⅛ teaspoon cayenne pepper

⅛ teaspoon freshly ground black pepper

1 cup (2 sticks) unsalted butter, at room temperature

1 cup packed light brown sugar

¾ cup granulated sugar

¾ cup chocolate-hazelnut spread (such as Nutella)

2 eggs

2 tablespoons fresh orange zest (from 1 large orange)

2 teaspoons espresso powder (see Sources, page 200)

1 teaspoon vanilla extract

1 cup bittersweet or semisweet chocolate chips

1⅓ cup pepitas (pumpkin seeds), toasted (see Note)

¼ cup cacao nibs (see Note)

{ continued }

PULSE the oats in a food processor until finely ground. Add the flour, cocoa powder, salt, baking soda, baking powder, cinnamon, cloves, cayenne, and black pepper. Pulse a few times to combine.

IN a stand mixer fitted with the paddle attachment, cream the butter and both sugars until light and fluffy. Add the chocolate-hazelnut spread, eggs, orange zest, espresso powder, and vanilla and beat until well blended. Add the dry ingredients and mix on low until just incorporated. Stir in the chocolate chips, ⅓ cup of the pepitas, and the cacao nibs. Refrigerate the dough in the bowl for at least 3 hours.

PREHEAT the oven to 350°F and lightly grease two baking sheets.

USE a ¼-cup measure or 4-tablespoon cookie scoop to drop dough rounds in batches on the prepared sheets 3 inches apart. Use your thumb to push down the centers midway into the cookie. (This makes for an even rise without a dome.) Top each cookie evenly with 1 teaspoon pepitas.

BAKE for 13 to 15 minutes, just until the dough doesn't have that wet look, but is still soft. Remove the cookies to a wire rack and let them cool for several minutes before serving. Store in an airtight container for up to 1 week.

NOTE Toast pepitas in a skillet, stirring occasionally, until light golden, or bake at 350°F, stirring occasionally, for about 10 minutes, until light golden.

Cacao nibs are roasted cacao bean pieces that have a nutty flavor and crunchy texture.

SWEET TALK "Texas is a state of mind. Texas is an obsession. Above all, Texas is a nation in every sense of the word."
—Author John Steinbeck

LAURA BUSH'S **COWBOY COOKIES**

MAKES ABOUT 36 LARGE COOKIES ★ No matter on which side of the political fence you stand, there's one thing that can't be argued: how good these cookies are. And, in size, what a handful they are—as big as a Texan's pride. The former First Lady of Texas and the United States cooked up these cookies for a *Family Circle* magazine voting contest in which she defeated Tipper Gore (her gingersnaps, that is). Fortunately there didn't need to be a re-count. These cookies are certainly fitting for when the Bushes entertain at their Prairie Chapel Ranch in Crawford, Texas, due west of Waco.

3 cups all-purpose flour

1 tablespoon baking powder

1 tablespoon baking soda

1 tablespoon ground cinnamon

1 teaspoon salt

1½ cups (3 sticks) unsalted butter, at room temperature

1½ cups granulated sugar

1½ cups packed light brown sugar

3 eggs

1 tablespoon vanilla extract

3 cups semisweet chocolate chips

3 cups old-fashioned rolled oats

2 cups flaked coconut

2 cups chopped pecans, lightly toasted (see Note, page 30)

PREHEAT the oven to 350°F.

IN a medium bowl, mix together the flour, baking powder, baking soda, cinnamon, and salt.

IN a stand mixer fitted with the paddle attachment, beat the butter on medium speed until smooth and creamy, about 1 minute. Gradually beat in both sugars to combine, about 2 minutes.

ADD the eggs, one at a time, beating after each addition. Beat in the vanilla.

STIR the flour mixture into the butter mixture until just combined. Add the chocolate chips, oats, coconut, and pecans and mix just to combine.

DROP the dough onto ungreased baking sheets using a ¼-cup measure or a 4-tablespoon cookie scoop, spacing the dough rounds 3 inches apart. Press down dough rounds slightly (to avoid domes from forming).

BAKE for about 12 minutes before rotating the sheets (to ensure even cooking). Bake another 8 to 12 minutes, or until the edges are lightly browned. Remove the cookies to wire racks to cool. Store in an airtight container for up to 1 week.

NOTE: To make six dozen smaller cookies, use 2 tablespoons dough for each cookie and bake for 15 to 18 minutes total, rotating midway through the cooking process.

SWEET TALK "Some folks look at me and see a certain swagger. In Texas it's called walking." —President George W. Bush

ALMOND LACE COOKIES

MAKES 48 COOKIES ☆ Memories have smells, you know. It's part of that whole sixth-sense thing. "Every time I bake these it brings back so many memories of my childhood," says Abilene mom Noelle Bledsoe. "I used to spend hours baking cookies with my grandmother in her kitchen. I can smell that memory now—how good everything tasted right out of the oven." Like these intricately laced old-fashioned cookies, which smell just as good coming out of my oven.

1 cup old-fashioned rolled oats

1 cup sugar

2 tablespoons all-purpose flour

½ teaspoon salt

¼ teaspoon baking powder

½ cup (1 stick) unsalted butter, melted

1 egg, lightly beaten

1 teaspoon vanilla extract

1½ cups sliced almonds

PREHEAT the oven to 325°F.

IN a large bowl, combine the oats, sugar, flour, salt, and baking powder.

IN a separate bowl, whisk the butter, egg, and vanilla together, then add to the dry ingredients. Add the almonds and stir until they are evenly distributed.

LINE a baking sheet with foil or parchment paper; coat lightly with nonstick baking spray.

DROP level teaspoons of dough 3 inches apart on the prepared sheet. Flatten slightly. Bake for 9 to 11 minutes, until they are golden brown. Let the cookies cool completely, then peel them off the foil. Store in an airtight container for about 1 week.

SWEET TALK Because these cookies are almost paper-thin at points, they will look like mistakes until you see how beautiful they are once peeled off the foil. Save any crumbles for ice cream.

DUTCH OVEN COBBLER
WITH BUTTERMILK-LIME ICE CREAM

SERVES 8 TO 10 ★ Fort Worth chef and author Grady Spears is the undisputed King of Cowboy Cooking. And he's the real deal: A former ranch hand who, moonlighting as a restaurant manager, wound up working as the head cook when the one there walked out. It's all part of what he calls "the cowboy code": "a respect for hard work, an understanding of the rhythms of nature, and appreciation of honest food." Though Grady's culinary roots stem from the chuck wagon, his fare runs more grand than grub. His easygoing gregarious personal style is as warm as his upscale Western restaurant Grady's, where the offerings are fresh, traditional, and unexpected. In the cobbler you can substitute other firm-fleshed fruits (such as cherries or apple slices).

BUTTERMILK-LIME ICE CREAM

1½ cups water

1½ cups sugar

3 cups buttermilk

1½ tablespoons light corn syrup

2 tablespoons fresh lime juice

1 tablespoon lime zest

⅛ teaspoon salt

COBBLER FILLING

4 cups fresh fruit (blackberries, sliced strawberries, blueberries) or chopped rhubarb

¾ cup sugar

3 tablespoons all-purpose flour

1½ cups water

1 tablespoon fresh lemon juice

2 tablespoons unsalted butter, melted

TENDER BUTTERMILK PASTRY

1¾ cups all-purpose flour

2 tablespoons sugar

2 tablespoons baking powder

1 teaspoon salt

¼ cup cold shortening

¼ cup plus 2 tablespoons heavy whipping cream

¼ cup plus 2 tablespoons buttermilk

3 tablespoons unsalted butter, melted

¼ cup sugar

1 tablespoon ground cinnamon

{ continued }

TO MAKE THE ICE CREAM: In a medium saucepan, bring the water and sugar to a boil. Remove the sugar syrup from the heat and refrigerate until cold.

IN a medium bowl, combine the sugar syrup with the buttermilk, corn syrup, lime juice, lime zest, and salt. Freeze in an ice-cream maker according to the manufacturer's directions. Pack the ice cream into a freezer container and freeze until firm, at least 20 minutes.

TO MAKE THE FILLING: Preheat the oven to 350°F.

PUT the fruit in a lightly greased 2½- to 3-quart Dutch oven, casserole, or baking pan.

IN a medium bowl, combine the sugar and flour. Add the water, lemon juice, and butter and mix well. Pour the mixture over the fruit. Bake for about 15 minutes, then increase the oven temperature to 425°F.

TO MAKE THE PASTRY: In a large bowl, stir to combine the flour, sugar, baking powder, and salt. Using a pastry blender or two forks, cut in the shortening, a little at a time, until the mixture resembles coarse meal. Stir in the cream and buttermilk and combine well.

REMOVE the dough to a lightly floured surface and knead four or five times, until it is smooth and glossy. Roll the dough out to about ¼ inch thick. Cut the dough to fit the baking dish.

PLACE the dough over the hot berries; brush the top with the melted butter.

BAKE for 20 to 30 minutes more, or until the pastry is golden brown.

BEFORE serving, combine the ¼ cup sugar and cinnamon, and sprinkle them over the hot cobbler. Serve with the ice cream.

SWEET TALK "If you don't have a Dutch oven, a favorite casserole dish or deep baking pan will do just fine," Grady says. Otherwise, "Just be sure to use the ripest berries for the best flavor."

Outdoor Cobbler Cooking

To cook this cobbler in the great outdoors: Assemble it in a cast-iron Dutch oven, cover, and cook directly over ten to twelve hot coals (with twelve to fourteen hot coals on top of the oven lid, placed there with long tongs) for 45 minutes to 1 hour. Just keep that ash out of the goods!

BLUEBERRY FRIED PIES

MAKES ABOUT TWELVE 3½-INCH PIES ★ Fresh summer fruit is best savored when eaten out of hand, and even sweeter when it's in a fried hand pie. Most of these hot pockets are made on a whim, so that's why I make them with ready-made refrigerated piecrusts (but use whatever you'd like). This treat is all about ease. Vanilla ice cream on the side completes the pretty picture.

¾ cup sugar, plus more for dusting

¼ cup cornstarch

2 cups fresh blueberries

1 tablespoon butter

One 15-ounce package refrigerated piecrust

Vegetable oil, for frying

Vanilla ice cream for serving (optional)

IN a large saucepan, mix the sugar and cornstarch until blended; add 1 cup water. Place the pan over medium heat and bring the mixture to a boil, stirring occasionally. Cook for about 2 minutes, or until thick and bubbly. Remove from the heat.

PUT the blueberries into a large bowl and pour the sugar mixture over them. Add the butter and mix well. Let the berries cool completely.

ROLL one sheet of piecrust on a lightly floured surface just enough to press out the fold lines. Cut the piecrust into nine or ten pieces with a 3-inch round or heart-shaped cutter. Roll out dough remnants and cut out two or three extra circles. Repeat with the other piecrust.

ROLL out each piecrust piece to a 3½-inch diameter and moisten the edges with water. Spoon 2 teaspoons (about 11 berries) of the blueberry mixture into the center of each. Top with another piecrust piece, pressing the edges together and then crimping with the tines of a fork to seal.

PUT the pies in a single layer on a baking sheet or layered with wax paper in a container, and freeze for at least 1 hour before frying.

{ continued }

POUR the vegetable oil to a depth of 1 inch into an electric frying pan, deep fryer, or skillet and heat to 360°F. Fry the pies directly from the freezer in batches for 1 to 2 minutes on each side, or until golden. Drain them on paper towels and dust with sugar just before serving, which is pretty much immediately, especially if you'll be having them with ice cream. Either way, eat them warm if you can.

SWEET TALK Freezing these sweethearts before frying prevents the piecrusts, with their weepy interiors, from falling apart in the hot oil. And, speaking of freezing, pre-fried, these can be stored for up to 1 month in an airtight container. You can even refreeze them after frying. The best way to reheat them is to defrost them for an hour or two in the refrigerator. Bake for 10 to 12 minutes in a 350°F oven, until warmed through. You also can heat them up in the microwave for about 1 minute, but I don't recommend that as much; their interiors will be explosively hot long before the exteriors will feel like the right temperature. And hey, you can even throw a few defrosted ones on the grill to heat up to your liking.

DEEP CHOCOLATE MERINGUE PIE

MAKES ONE 9-INCH PIE ★ Neva Everidge, the twelfth of thirteen children, grew up in West Texas in the early 1900s. "Mother loved to eat, and she really loved chocolate," recalls her daughter, Texas cooking historian Patricia Mitchell (who oversees TexasCooking.com with her son). "She cooked with quantities of butter and cream, was never overweight, and lived to be eighty-six. Not bad."

"I definitely prefer the standard (shortening) pastry with this pie," Patricia says. "You want nothing to detract from or interfere with the chocolate. Butter pastry is good, but I find it heavier and not as flaky."

FILLING

1¼ cups sugar, or more to taste

½ cup unsweetened cocoa powder

½ cup all-purpose flour

¼ teaspoon salt

4 egg yolks (reserve whites for meringue)

2 cups whole or 2% milk

1 teaspoon vanilla extract

PERFECT MERINGUE

4 egg whites

¼ teaspoon cream of tartar

6 tablespoons sugar

½ teaspoon vanilla extract

Standard Pie Pastry (page 169), fully baked, or one 9-inch baked piecrust

{ continued }

PREHEAT the oven to 350°F.

TO MAKE THE FILLING: In a medium bowl, sift together the sugar, cocoa powder, flour, and salt. Set aside.

ADD the egg yolks to a heavy medium saucepan and whisk well. Stir in the sifted dry ingredients alternately with the milk, adding a little at a time to keep the mixture smooth.

COOK over medium heat, adding the vanilla when it begins to bubble. Simmer, stirring constantly, until the mixture thickens, about 2 minutes. Remove from the heat; beat out any lumps that may have formed. Set aside. (Immediately proceed to the next step to ensure pie filling is still warm when meringue tops it, see Sweet Talk.)

TO MAKE THE MERINGUE: In a stand mixer fitted with the whisk attachment, beat the egg whites at high speed until soft peaks form. With the mixer running, add the cream of tartar. Gradually add the sugar, 1 tablespoon at a time, and beat until stiff, glossy peaks form. Beat in the vanilla.

POUR the warm custard into the piecrust and pile the meringue atop the filling, stopping just shy of the rim. Bake for 12 to 15 minutes, until the meringue is lightly browned.

LET the pie cool on a wire rack for at least 3 hours or invert a large bowl over it (the edges shouldn't touch the meringue) and refrigerate overnight before serving.

SWEET TALK To create a good "seal" between layers and to avoid a "weeping" meringue, do not allow the filling to cool before topping with the meringue. Also, meringue pies cut more easily with a wet knife blade. And another thing: Don't do what a *Southern Living* reader once told me she'd done when calling to complain about a recipe: She'd used tartar *sauce* instead of cream of tartar. She said, "But they're the same thing … right?" No.

PATRICIA'S PIECRUSTS

MAKES ENOUGH PASTRY FOR ONE 9-INCH, SINGLE-CRUST PIE ★ Patricia Mitchell has two go-to crust recipes—one made with butter and the other made with vegetable shortening. "Remember, the less you work the dough, the lighter and flakier the pastry," Patricia advises. "Conventional wisdom holds, and I agree, that glass (Pyrex) pie plates generally make better piecrusts than those made of metal," she adds. (Glass helps conduct the heat more evenly, allowing the bottom of the pie to bake thoroughly.) For a 9-inch double- or lattice-crust pie, just double these recipes.

BUTTER PASTRY

1¼ cups all-purpose flour

¼ teaspoon salt

1 teaspoon sugar

½ cup (1 stick) cold unsalted butter, cut into small pieces

¼ cup ice water

PUT the flour, salt, and sugar in a food processor. Pulse a few times to mix.

ADD the butter pieces and process for about 10 seconds, until the mixture is the consistency of coarse meal.

WITH the food processor running, slowly add the ice water in a thin stream just until the dough holds together. Do not process the dough for more than half a minute. (To hand-mix the dough, follow the method for Standard Pie Pastry [facing page], sprinkling the ice water on and mixing until the dough holds together.)

TURN the dough out, roll it into a ball, and wrap it securely in plastic wrap. Refrigerate for 1 hour before rolling out.

FOR a prebaked piecrust, prick the bottom and sides of the pastry with a fork and add pie weights to avoid bubbles developing, and bake in a 425°F oven for 10 to 12 minutes, until the crust is lightly browned. Remove the crust to a wire rack to cool before filling.

STANDARD PIE PASTRY

1⅓ cups all-purpose flour

½ teaspoon salt

½ cup shortening

3 tablespoons ice water

SIFT together the flour with the salt; set aside.

PUT the shortening in a medium bowl. Over it, pour the flour-salt mixture. With your pastry blender (traditionalists use two forks), cut the flour and salt into the shortening until the mixture resembles coarse meal.

ADD the ice water, 1 tablespoon at a time, stirring the dough around with a fork. As soon as it is moist enough, roll it into a ball, wrap it in wax paper, and refrigerate it for about 30 minutes. (Handle the dough as little as possible to keep it from becoming tough.)

ON a lightly floured work surface, roll the dough 2 to 3 inches wider than a 9-inch pie plate and about ⅛ inch thick.

CENTER the dough on the pie plate and fit the dough into the plate without stretching it. (If the dough tears a little, just pinch it back together.)

TRIM the dough to overhang the edge of the pie plate by at least 1½ inches, then turn the dough under to make an edge. You can put a fancy crimp in the edge at this point, if you wish. The unbaked crust can be kept covered and refrigerated for up to 1 week before baking.

FOR a prebaked piecrust, prick the bottom and sides of the pastry with a fork and add pie weights to avoid bubbles developing, and bake in a 425°F oven for 10 to 12 minutes, until the crust is lightly browned. Remove the crust to a wire rack to cool before filling.

NOTE: Either piecrust may be frozen, wrapped in wax paper, and sealed in an airtight container for up to 3 months.

PERINI RANCH **STRAWBERRY SHORTCAKES**

SERVES 12 ⭐ When I think of a Texan through and through, pure and simple, and smart as a whip, I see Tom Perini of Buffalo Gap, a tiny town not far from Abilene—and old Comanche country. I see the "Ambassador of West Texas" (as dubbed by a classic radio station) milling about in jeans, a denim shirt, and ivory cowboy hat. He's ambling around on his 640-acre family ranch that he's helped tend since boyhood. He's checking in on his famous peppered beef tenderloin smoking over mesquite at the venerable bunkhouse-style Perini Steakhouse, showing guests the authentic chuck wagon parked out back, happily signing copies of his iconic book, *Texas Cowboy Cooking*, working the cattle during the day, and kicking back on one of the patios at sunset, talking about what's good in life and meaning every sincere gesture or word. I also think of this recipe—his mother's actually—which is as no-nonsense and sweet as Tom. Hats off to keeping it real, sir.

TOM'S BUTTERMILK SHORTCAKES

2½ cups soft-wheat or 2¼ cups all-purpose flour

1½ tablespoons sugar

2 teaspoons baking powder

¾ teaspoon salt

½ teaspoon baking soda

5 tablespoons cold shortening or lard (for a flakier shortcake)

1 cup buttermilk

FILLING AND TOPPING

4 cups hulled ripe, fresh strawberries

¾ cup sugar

1 cup heavy whipping cream

Garnish: Small fresh strawberries (optional)

TO MAKE THE SHORTCAKES: Preheat the oven to 450°F.

IN a large bowl, sift together the flour, sugar, baking powder, salt, and baking soda. Sift several times to combine the ingredients.

CUT the shortening into the flour mixture with two forks or a pastry blender until the dough is the texture of coarse meal. Add the buttermilk and mix just until the dough comes together. (It will be sticky.)

PUT the dough on a well-floured work surface and knead about five times. Roll it out or pat it to ½ inch thick. Use a biscuit cutter or tin can to cut the dough into 2½- to 3-inch rounds; place them on an ungreased baking sheet. Use your thumb to push the biscuit centers one-fourth of the way down. (This will make for a dome-free rise.)

BAKE for 10 to 12 minutes, depending on size, until they are a light golden brown. Remove the shortcakes to a wire rack to cool slightly.

TO MAKE THE FILLING AND TOPPING: Cut the strawberries in half lengthwise; put them in a large bowl. Sprinkle the strawberries with ½ cup of the sugar and let them sit at room temperature until the fruit begins to produce juice, about 1 hour.

PUT the strawberries and juice in a large saucepan and warm thoroughly over very low heat, stirring occasionally and gently, just until the mixture begins to thicken, about 20 minutes.

IN a chilled metal bowl, whip the cream and remaining ¼ cup sugar (with cold beaters) on high for 3 to 4 minutes, until stiff peaks form.

SLICE each shortcake in half, placing the bottom portion on a plate. Spoon 2 tablespoons of the strawberry mixture onto each plated shortcake. Place the top half of the shortcake on and cover with another 1 tablespoon strawberries. Top with a dollop of whipped cream. Garnish with a small berry, if desired, and serve.

SWEET TALK "Make the shortcakes for your morning breakfast, and you'll have enough left over for dessert that evening," says Tom. Sounds like a fine idea to me.

CHERRY DR PEPPER CUPCAKES

MAKES ABOUT 36 CUPCAKES ★ This is my ode to the Dr Pepper Supper Cake, which is just as traditional to Texas as the Coca-Cola cake is to Georgia. The cake, or here, the cupcake, tastes even better over time, with each day of ownership (up to five days' time) offering a fuller hint of Dr Pepper flavor. Cherry-flavored Dr Pepper adds just a wee more cherry flavoring to this recipe, but otherwise, both varieties work just fine. The sour cream provides a glorious moistness, and the festive cherry–cream cheese frosting gives an added dose of refreshment.

CUPCAKES

2¼ cups cherry-flavored or regular Dr Pepper

½ cup maraschino cherry syrup

⅔ cup unsalted butter

½ cup unsweetened cocoa powder

1½ cups granulated sugar

½ cup sour cream

1½ teaspoons ground cinnamon

1 teaspoon baking soda

1 teaspoon baking powder

1 teaspoon vanilla extract

⅛ teaspoon salt

2½ cups all-purpose flour

2 eggs, lightly beaten

FLUFFY CHERRY-CREAM CHEESE FROSTING

½ cup heavy whipping cream

8 ounces cream cheese, at room temperature

½ cup (1 stick) unsalted butter, at room temperature

1 tablespoon vanilla extract

3 cups powdered sugar, sifted

¼ cup cherry preserves

Garnish: Candy sprinkles, maraschino cherries

{ continued }

TO MAKE THE CUPCAKES: Preheat the oven to 325°F and line three dozen cupcake cups with paper liners.

IN a medium saucepan, bring the Dr Pepper and cherry syrup to a boil.

IN a medium bowl, combine the butter and cocoa powder and pour the hot syrup mixture over it. Cover and let sit for 10 minutes before whisking the mixture smooth.

STIR in the granulated sugar, sour cream, cinnamon, baking soda, baking powder, vanilla, and salt.

ADD the flour in two parts, alternating with the eggs, and whisk till smooth. The mixture will be runny, but that's okay.

FILL the prepared cups two-thirds full and bake for 15 to 20 minutes, or until a toothpick inserted into the center of the cakes comes out clean. Let the cupcakes cool in the pans for 10 to 12 minutes, then remove them to wire racks to cool completely.

TO MAKE THE FROSTING: In a chilled metal bowl, whip the cream (with cold beaters) on high speed for 3 to 4 minutes, until stiff peaks form. Remove the whipped cream to a separate smaller bowl (preferably chilled, to help keep it fluffy) and set aside.

ADD the cream cheese, butter, and vanilla to the mixing bowl and beat until smooth. Gradually add the powdered sugar. Beat until spreadable. Fold in the preserves and reserved whipped cream and gently stir to combine. Refrigerate for at least 1 hour.

FROST the cooled cupcakes, and garnish with candy sprinkles or maraschino cherries, if desired. Store in a baking pan covered with tented plastic wrap or foil— or better yet, a portable covered cupcake container— for 1 day unrefrigerated or up to 1 week refrigerated.

SWEET TALK Ever see those small, old-timey glass bottles of Dr Pepper touted as being from Dublin, Texas? Grab 'em. They're the original formula, which uses Imperial pure cane sugar made at the oldest Dr Pepper bottler in the world. You really can savor the difference. For an ordering source, see page 200.

Dr Feelgood: A Sip of Dr Pepper History

Dublin, Texas—halfway between Abilene and Fort Worth—is the birthplace of Dr Pepper's first and oldest bottling plant, founded in 1891 to produce what actually was created in Waco, Texas, six years earlier. The drink, initially a soda fountain syrup with fruit, spice, and berry aromas, was invented by pharmacist Charles Alderton to re-create the exuberant flavors that intermingled at the fountain. This all happened at Wade Morrison's Old Corner Drug Store, and Morrison decided to name the drink "Dr Pepper" in honor of the father of the girlfriend he'd left behind in his home state of Virginia. (By the way, the period was removed from the "Dr" in the 1950s to make it more graphically pleasing to the eye.)

By 1891, Morrison and a partner had founded the Artesian Manufacturing and Bottling Company to sell the soft drink, and soon another bottling outpost popped up eighty miles west in Dublin. The drink's popularity spread quickly but it didn't reach a fever pitch until the world was officially introduced to it at the 1904 World's Fair in St. Louis. And though the Dr Pepper brand is now a worldwide sensation and bottled far and wide, the Dublin bottling plant is still going strong—but with a unique twist: It still makes the original sweeter version of the soft drink, which featured pure cane sugar instead of the less-expensive fructose corn syrup used now. Tours of the working antique bottling line are available at the Dublin plant and there's also a museum of collectibles and a memorabilia shop. (Meanwhile, the Waco museum focuses more

on the old drugstore and the soft-drink industry in general.) For more details visit OldDocs.com.

Lil' trivia: What do the "10," "2," and "4" numbers signify on old Dr Pepper bottle labels, clock faces, and the like? Those were the times of the day when it was discovered (by Dr. Walter Eddy of Columbia University) that the human body needed a little pick-me-up to avoid energy slumps. The Dr Pepper brand jumped on that notion, suggesting with a revamped logo that it offered just the "pep" a person needed during those time frames.

GOOD OL' TEXAS SHEET CAKE

MAKES ONE 10-×-15-INCH CAKE ★ If there's a quintessential Texas dessert, this, my friends, is it. This is the one everybody takes to a family reunion or church social or what have you. (It's also not uncommon to see five or six of these on one banquet table.) Making it is as easy as breathing. They're also less showy, like most people in our great state. (OK, I said *most*.) The main thing to know is that the batter will be thin, but no worries: The cake will turn out moist and perfect, especially when that icing gets on top and on in there.

THE CAKE

2 cups granulated sugar

2 cups all-purpose flour

1/2 to 1 teaspoon ground cinnamon (optional)

1 cup (2 sticks) unsalted butter

5 tablespoons unsweetened cocoa powder

1 cup water

1/2 cup buttermilk

2 eggs, lightly beaten

1 teaspoon baking soda

1 teaspoon vanilla extract

THE ICING

1/2 cup (1 stick) unsalted butter

6 tablespoons milk

5 tablespoons unsweetened cocoa powder

3²/₃ cups powdered sugar, sifted

1/2 cup finely chopped pecans, lightly toasted (see Note, page 30)

1 teaspoon vanilla extract

{ continued }

TO MAKE THE CAKE: Preheat the oven to 400°F and lightly grease and flour a 10-×-15-×-1-inch baking (jelly-roll) pan.

IN a large bowl, sift together the granulated sugar, flour, and cinnamon (if using).

IN a medium saucepan, bring the butter, cocoa powder, and water just to a boil over medium-high heat, stirring constantly; pour over the sugar mixture. Stir well to thoroughly combine.

STIR the buttermilk into the mixture. Add the eggs, baking soda, and vanilla and stir well to thoroughly combine.

POUR the batter into the prepared pan and bake for 20 to 25 minutes, until a toothpick inserted near the center comes out clean.

TO MAKE THE ICING: In a medium saucepan, bring the butter, milk, and cocoa powder to a boil, stirring constantly. Remove from the heat and add the powdered sugar, pecans, and vanilla; mix well for a smooth texture.

REMOVE the cake pan to a wire rack for 1 or 2 minutes. Pour the hot icing over the hot cake and spread evenly. Allow the iced cake to cool in the pan on a wire rack before serving. Cover leftovers with plastic wrap and keep refrigerated for up to 1 week.

SWEET TALK Former First Lady Lady Bird Johnson is thought to have introduced our great nation to this chocolate buttermilk cake as her "Mexican Chocolate Cake" back in the early 1960s. But because it spreads out wide and flat, it soon became the "Texas" cake. (Actually it's similar to Georgia's famed Coca-Cola cake—which substitutes Coke for the water and/or buttermilk.) Now, as for which one came first, many believe ours did, since there are references to similar cakes from the late 1930s. The later-arriving Coca-Cola cake had to be inspired by somethin', right? I'm just sayin'.

Sheet vs. Sheath: It's All Good

Most call this a "sheet" cake but many Texans in the western and northern reaches of the state call it a "sheath" cake. No one has any idea why, other than perhaps at some point someone misunderstood "sheath" for "sheet" and that was all she wrote. This reminds me of the whole Southern "roulage" business (when, in essence, it's "roulade"). The truth of the matter is that it doesn't really matter. Good is good.

GRANDMOTHER SHAUGHNESSY'S
LEMON SPONGE CAKE

MAKES ONE 9½-INCH CAKE ☆ Renowned Wool & Hoop crewel artist and author Katherine Shaughnessy is one of the many creative types who call Marfa home. She and her family are in Big Bend country, majestic in its mountains, caverns, and prairie meadows. But the arid, high-altitude climate poses a conundrum if you like to bake. Which she does. "Apparently there's something scientific about using a Bundt or angel food cake pan that helps give cakes more lift," says Katherine, who's tried many a cake recipe to find just the right one. "This one's foolproof. All the others want to fall." What a gift her grandmother continues to bequeath—a light and lemony old-fashioned cake that's as soulful to savor as Marfa's big, intensely golden-pink sunsets.

LEMON SPONGE CAKE

7 eggs, separated, at room temperature (see Note)

½ teaspoon cream of tartar

¼ teaspoon salt

1 cup granulated sugar

2½ tablespoons fresh lemon juice

1 cup cake flour (see Note)

LEMON CREAM ICING

½ cup (1 stick) unsalted butter, at room temperature

3⅔ cups powdered sugar

¼ cup heavy whipping cream

1 teaspoon vanilla extract

1 teaspoon fresh lemon juice

⅛ teaspoon salt

SWEET TALK To cool this cake, Katherine does what her grandmother did: Set the cake on a riser of overturned coffee cups.

TO MAKE THE CAKE: Preheat the oven to 350°F. Have an ungreased 9½-×-4-inch angel food (tube) cake pan ready.

IN a large bowl, use a mixer to whip the egg whites until frothy. Whisk in the cream of tartar and salt. Beat just until soft peaks form. Gradually add ½ cup of the granulated sugar. Whip again until stiff, glossy peaks form (but aren't dry).

IN a larger bowl, use a mixer to beat the egg yolks until thick. Slowly add the lemon juice and remaining ½ cup granulated sugar. Beat until the mixture is well combined. Gently stir in the flour.

FOLD one-fourth of the egg white mixture into the egg yolk mixture before folding all of the egg yolk mixture back into the egg white mixture.

POUR the batter into the cake pan.

BAKE for 35 minutes, or until the cake is golden and a toothpick inserted near the center comes out clean.

INVERT the pan onto a wire rack and let the cake cool completely (at least 3 hours) in the pan.

RUN a thin-bladed knife up and down around the edges of the cake as well as around the center tube. Gently lift the cake from the pan by the tube. Then run a knife under the cake to release it from the bottom.

PLACE the cake on a serving plate and refrigerate until cold (the icing will adhere better on a cold cake).

TO MAKE THE ICING: In a large bowl, place the butter and slowly add the powdered sugar while whisking on low speed until well combined. Slowly add the cream, vanilla, lemon juice, and salt. Whisk on high until the icing is light and fluffy.

ICE the entire cold cake with a very thin layer of icing. Let it sit for 5 minutes.

ICE the entire cake again so none of the cake underneath can be seen. Store the cake at room temperature beneath a cake cover if planning to eat within a day, or refrigerate, tented with plastic wrap, for up to 3 days. Let the cake return to room temperature (this takes about 1 hour) before serving.

NOTE Let chilled egg whites stand at room temperature for 30 minutes before using or fit a bowl of whites atop another bowl of hot (but not boiling) water to warm them up while beating.

For high-altitude baking, Katherine substitutes the same amount of all-purpose flour for the cake flour to provide more structure (though in lower elevations, the substitution should be ¾ cup plus 2 tablespoons of all-purpose flour for 1 cup of cake flour).

BABE'S BANANA CAKE
WITH CREAMY NUT FROSTING

MAKES ONE 9-INCH DOUBLE-LAYER CAKE ★ Babe Hodges Shepherd Senna carved out quite a life for herself thanks to a talent for singing, which she and sisters Grace, Fannibelle, and Hallie (a.k.a. "Happy") shared while performing as the girl group the Hodges Sisters. (Babe later went on to tour with big bands.) She hailed from Newlin, a wide spot in the Panhandle near Turkey, Texas—home to, not only, the great "King of Western Swing," Bob Wills, but also to an early preponderance of wild turkeys. Besides turning heads with her voice as well as her good looks (a mix of Irish and Osage Sioux—see her on page 2), she also found harmony in the kitchen, baking such old-time cakes as this one. "This cake is pure Panhandle Texas," says my SMU colleague Kathleen Tibbetts, who inherited her grandmother Babe's flair for baking.

BANANA CAKE

2 cups all-purpose flour

¾ teaspoon baking soda

½ teaspoon baking powder

½ teaspoon salt

1 cup granulated sugar

½ cup shortening

2 eggs

1 teaspoon vanilla extract

3 bananas, mashed (about 1¼ cups)

½ cup buttermilk

½ cup chopped pecans (optional)

CREAMY NUT FROSTING

½ cup milk

2½ tablespoons all-purpose flour

½ cup shortening

½ cup granulated sugar

¼ teaspoon salt

1 teaspoon vanilla extract

1 cup powdered sugar

½ chopped pecans or walnuts, toasted (see Note, page 30)

{ continued }

TO MAKE THE CAKE: Preheat the oven to 350°F and grease and flour two 9-inch round cake pans.

IN a medium bowl, sift together the flour, baking soda, baking powder, and salt. Set aside.

IN a large bowl, combine the granulated sugar, shortening, eggs, and vanilla. Beat with a hand mixer on high until fluffy. Turn the mixer down to medium and alternate adding the mashed bananas and flour mixture (about ½ cup at a time), mixing well after each addition.

ADD the buttermilk last and all at once; mix until well combined. The batter should look fluffy and hold its shape slightly. Fold in the pecans (if using).

DIVIDE the batter between the prepared pans. Tap the pans on the counter or other hard surface to distribute the batter evenly and to knock out any large air bubbles. Bake for 27 to 30 minutes, or until a toothpick inserted in the center comes out clean. Cool the cakes on wire racks in the pans for 10 minutes, then remove from the pans and allow to cool completely on the racks.

TO MAKE THE FROSTING: Whisk together the milk and flour in a saucepan and cook over low heat until very thick and smooth, stirring constantly for 5 to 7 minutes, without letting the paste brown. Remove from the heat and let cool for about 10 minutes.

IN the bowl of a stand mixer fitted with the paddle attachment, cream the shortening, granulated sugar, and salt on high speed until fluffy. Add the flour paste and vanilla; beat until smooth. Add the powdered sugar ⅓ cup at a time, mixing well on low with each addition. Beat on high for 1 or 2 minutes, or until fluffy. Fold in the nuts (or sprinkle them atop the cake as a garnish).

PUT one cake layer on a plate or cake stand and spread with about 1/2 cup of the frosting. Top with the other layer. Spread the remaining frosting on the top and sides of the cake. Store the cake at room temperature beneath a cake cover if planning to eat within a day, or refrigerate, tented with plastic wrap, for up to 3 days. Let the cake return to room temperature (this takes about 1 hour) before serving.

SWEET TALK "To get the light cake texture and smooth icing you want, it's important not to skip any steps," says Kathleen. "The result definitely will reward the effort."

Web Feat:
TexasCooking.com

Many traditional state recipes can be found on TexasCooking.com, a well-stocked site that Patricia Mitchell and her son Steve Labinski created in 1997—way back before cooking on the Web was cool—for sharing recipes and cultivating stories about Texas cooking. Drop by sometime. And note that they also sell an impressive array of Fiestaware, which makes old-time pies that much more authentic.

TRES LECHES CAKE

MAKES ONE 9-×-13-INCH CAKE ★ This cake never fails to brighten a meal's end. The Latin American "three milks" sponge cake is rich, sweet, soft, cool, light, and fluffy. Its lack of butter lets the milk do the plumping, leaving it creamy and not soggy. It's simple and gracious. Just like a Texan.

1 cup all-purpose flour

1½ teaspoons baking powder

¼ teaspoon salt

5 eggs, separated

1 cup plus 3 tablespoons sugar

⅓ cup whole milk

1 to 2 teaspoons vanilla extract

One 14-ounce can sweetened condensed milk

One 12-ounce can evaporated milk

2¼ cups heavy whipping cream

Garnish: Fresh fruit slices (optional)

PREHEAT the oven to 350°F. Coat a 9-×-13-inch pan with baking spray and set aside.

IN a large bowl, combine the flour, baking powder, and salt.

IN a stand mixer fitted with the whisk attachment, beat the egg yolks with ¾ cup of the sugar on high speed until the yolks are pale yellow. Stir in the milk and 1 teaspoon vanilla to combine. Pour the mixture over the flour mixture and gently stir until combined.

IN the clean bowl of a stand mixer fitted with a clean whisk attachment, beat the egg whites on high speed until soft peaks form. With the mixer still running, add ¼ cup of the sugar and beat until stiff, glossy peaks form (but aren't dry).

GENTLY fold the egg white mixture into the batter until just combined. Pour into the prepared pan and spread evenly.

BAKE for 35 to 45 minutes, or until a toothpick inserted into the center comes out clean.

LOOSEN the edges of the cake from the pan with a knife before removing it and placing the cake on a rimmed platter. Let the cake cool completely.

{ continued }

PIERCE the surface of the cake with fork tines or an ice/chocolate chipper (see Sources, page 200) or wooden skewer.

IN a bowl with a spout, combine the condensed milk, evaporated milk, and ¼ cup of the cream. Slowly drizzle all but about 1 cup of the mixture onto the cake, working to get much of it absorbed into the more-done edges.

ALLOW the cake to absorb the milk mixture for 30 minutes.

IN a chilled medium bowl, whip the remaining 2 cups cream (with cold beaters) with the remaining 3 tablespoons sugar until thick and spreadable (with a soft peak). See if you'd like to add vanilla, and if so, start with ½ teaspoon and go up to 1 teaspoon. Spread the mixture over the surface of the cake. Decorate the cake with fresh fruit, if desired.

LET the cake sit for at least 3 hours in the refrigerator before eating it. Cover and refrigerate leftovers for up to 1 week.

SWEET TALK Whole *tres leches* cakes look lovely lined with slices of strawberries, kiwis, and star fruit. As for adding the ubiquitous cherries, you can go there if you like, but that style reminds me of uninspired supermarket cakes. Be creative or just keep it simple.

Sweetened Condensed Milk: Borden's Can-Do Spirit

Texans are quite fond of sweetened condensed milk, and probably instantly picture it with a Borden's Eagle Brand label. (You know, the one with Elsie the cow.) There's a good reason for that.

The man behind the label is New Yorker Gail Borden (1801–1874), who moved through a series of career hits and misses—mostly misses—until making his way to the promising Republic of Texas in the early 1830s.

After a brief surveying stint in San Felipe (west of Houston), the former schoolteacher found firmer footing publishing the newspaper *Telegraph and Texas Register*, which focused on Texas's struggle for independence (and was the first to list the names of those who died at the Alamo). This position led him to help write the Republic of Texas's first constitution and also create the immense territory's first topographical map in 1835. He also dabbled in real estate, helping sell 2,500 lots on Galveston Island (the largest city in Texas during the latter half of the nineteenth century).

But it was Borden's interest in science that made him a famous man. After seeing several children die in 1851 from bad milk given to them on a ship traveling from England to the United States, he committed himself to finding a way to make what he called "the perfect food" portable (refrigeration was scarce to non-existent) and safe (this was pre-pasteurization). By 1856, he'd figured out how to condense milk through a vacuum process and won U.S. and British patents for the technique. It wasn't until the Civil War, though, that the need for portable milk took off, and Borden returned north to work with willing investors and canners. And he became as rich as the milk itself, which became popular across the globe.

Borden returned to Texas and died in the Panhandle city of Borden, where he'd established a meat packing plant. Soon afterward, the county was renamed Borden County and its county seat, rechristened Gail.

Borden's original copper kettle "vacuum pan" is now housed at the Smithsonian's National Museum of American History.

STRONG COFFEE CUSTARD

SERVES 6 ★ Some of my favorite coffee and conversation has been enjoyed at the family-run Good Luck Café in El Paso, home to the region's best *menudo* (the tripe soup that's good luck for hangover headaches). Thinking of the place reminds me of a story about coffee that I once heard there. "You know how cowboys tell when a big pot of coffee's ready, dontcha?" a fellow diner once asked with sly smile. "They throw a horseshoe in it. If it don't sink, it's ready to drink." OK, all right, we'll play along. The thing is, Texans *do* like their coffee strong. No colored water for us, thank you. Here's a light, fluffy, and chocolatey homage to keeping that horseshoe afloat.

2½ cups heavy whipping cream

8 egg yolks

¼ cup superfine sugar (see Sweet Talk)

½ cup strong brewed coffee (see Note)

¾ cup chopped good-quality bittersweet or semisweet chocolate

2 teaspoons unflavored gelatin

Garnish: Whipped cream, chocolate shavings

{ continued }

IN a medium saucepan, heat the cream over low for about 4 minutes, or until hot (do not boil).

IN a large bowl, whisk the egg yolks and sugar to combine. Very slowly whisk in the hot cream, whisking constantly until both mixtures are well combined. Pour the custard mixture back into the saucepan. Cook over low heat, stirring constantly, for 15 to 20 minutes, or until the custard thickens and just begins to bubble.

COMBINE the coffee and chocolate in a heat-proof, microwave-safe bowl. Microwave, uncovered, on high for 1 to 2 minutes, stirring every minute until melted and smooth. Stir into the custard mixture.

IN a small, microwave-safe bowl, whisk the gelatin and 1 tablespoon water to combine. Microwave, uncovered, on high for 30 seconds or until melted. Whisk until the mixture is clear. Stir the warm gelatin into the warm coffee custard.

POUR the custard into six 2/3-cup ramekins and cover with plastic wrap. Refrigerate for 6 to 8 hours, or until set. Garnish with whipped cream and chocolate curls, if desired, and serve.

NOTE To make strong coffee, make a small batch and increase the scoop to 1½ times what you'd normally use, or about one-quarter more coffee beans than you'd normally grind. You could also combine 4 teaspoons espresso powder into ½ cup boiling water.

SWEET TALK Superfine sugar allows for quick absorption and a less grainy texture than granulated sugar. If you don't want to pay more for it, use a coffee grinder or small food processor to break down the regular chunkier version into a finer product. Just let the sugar dust settle for a few minutes before opening up the holding container; you'll be glad you did.

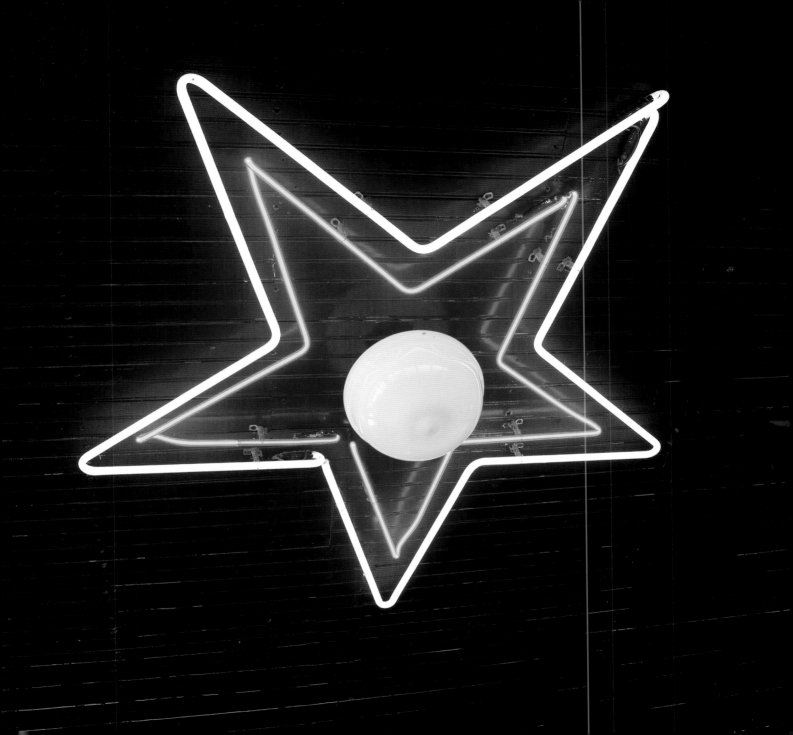

WATERMELON SOUP OOH LA LAH

SERVES 4 ★ Ellise Pierce grew up in Denton, Texas, eating summertime watermelon "so big you'd have to put it in a wheelbarrow to get it to the garage," which is where the green gourd with tiger stripes would go, in a big cooler of ice, she says. "We ate melon simply, with salt to bring out the flavor. And on white paper plates, always outside, because it was such a big mess," she remembers. Now the girl has up and left us to live in Paris. As in Gay Pair-ree, not the Lone Star's Paris. (Though she does make it home often to see family.) Her well-received blog, Cowgirl Chef, about life there has led to a book, *Cowgirl Chef: Cooking in Paris with a Texas Accent.* Summers in France, she says, afford virtually no air-conditioning, "and it does get warm in July and August," she notes. "So we do what we can to cool off: Drink rosé instead of red wine and start or end a meal with a cold soup, which are always on summer menus all over Paris." This version is her tribute to growing up in Denton.

SOUP

½ small seedless watermelon
(about 4 cups pulp and juice)

Sea salt

Sugar (optional)

CINNAMON WHIPPED CREAM

⅔ cup heavy whipping cream

3 tablespoons sugar

⅛ teaspoon ground cinnamon

Garnish: Ground cinnamon

{ continued }

TO MAKE THE SOUP: Cut the watermelon into 4-inch chunks and puree them in batches in a blender. Add a pinch of sea salt per batch and taste for seasoning; it may need a hint of sugar, depending on ripeness.

POUR the soup into a gallon-size zip-top plastic bag and refrigerate for at least 2 hours, or until well chilled.

TO MAKE THE WHIPPED CREAM: In a chilled metal bowl, whip the cream (with cold beaters). When it begins to thicken (after 3 minutes), slowly add the sugar and cinnamon. Keep mixing until soft peaks form.

DIVIDE the soup into four shallow bowls and top each with a generous dollop of whipped cream. Garnish each bowl with a dash of ground cinnamon, if desired, and serve.

SWEET TALK Two things to know: Salt "is the secret to making watermelon even sweeter," Ellise says. Oh, "and this makes enough cinnamon whipped cream for leftovers," she says. "I like mine spooned atop my coffee."

Come Get You Some: Top Twenty Texas Treats

There are many, many places that sell their goodies to the public, but these are my go-to spots for gift giving:

AUSTINUTS, Austin: Jalapeño peanut brittle, jelly beans galore, and lots more fun stuff. *AustiNuts.com* or 877-329-6887.

COLLIN STREET BAKERY, Corsicana: Delicious fruitcakes, bite-size fruitcake petites, pecan cakes, and cherry icebox cookies; in business since 1896. *CollinStreet.com* or 800-267-4657.

DELICIOUS TAMALES, San Antonio: Coconut, raisin, and pecan tamales are *delicioso*. That's why they sell more than two million tamales of all kinds annually. *DeliciousTamales.com* or 800-826-2531.

JANIE'S POUND CAKES, Tyler: Scrumptious pound cakes in eight flavors, including "The (Chocolate) Chipper Jane" in lovely yellow-and-white-striped boxes. *JaniesCakes.com* or 866-452-6437.

LAMMES CANDIES, Austin: Texas Chewy Pecan Pralines, nutty Choc'Adillos, and gift boxes; in business since 1885. *Lammes.com* or 800-252-1885.

LILY'S COOKIES, San Antonio: The cutest cookies anywhere (see photo at left). *LilysCookies.com* or 210-832-0886.

LINDALE CANDY CO., Lindale: They make supreme old-fashioned candies like candy canes and lollipops, sixteen flavors of fudge, and more. 866-894-2605.

MARY LOUISE BUTTERS BROWNIES, Austin: Unbelievable goodness and delightfully surprising flavors ("Seriously Stout" or "Mental Julep" anyone?). And "Brownie Butts" (end pieces), too. *ButtersBrownies.com* or 800-975-6309.

MARY OF PUDDIN' HILL, Greenville: Enjoy habanero peanut brittle and bite-size "little Puds" mini pies and fruitcakes. *PuddinHill.com* or 800-545-8889.

MILLICAN PECAN CO., San Saba: Since 1888 they've been crafting pecan confections. Their pecan pies are outstanding; they even make a Butterfinger pecan pie. *PecanCompany.com* or 866-484-6358.

MI TIERRA CAFÉ Y PANADERÍA, San Antonio: The very best in Mexican candy and gift boxes. *Giftshop.MiTierraCafe.com* or 800-360-1638.

NEIMAN MARCUS, Dallas and beyond: Yes, they do mail-order—for gorgeous peppermint butter cookies, cookie assortments, 24K S'mores Hearts, and, of course, their famous chocolate chip cookies. *NeimanMarcus.com* or 888-888-4757.

ORIGINAL CAKE BALL CO., Dallas: These tiny truffle-style cakes are delectable. *CakeBalls.com* or 214-559-5788.

THE PIE QUEEN'S CUTIE PIES, Austin: Amazing little 4-inch pies, especially the buttermilk ones and white chocolate–coconut-pecan. *CutiePieWagon.com* or 512-452-7437.

ROSCAR BONBONS AND COUNTRY TRUFFLES, Bastrop: Excellent chocolates in fun flavors and designs, including Pumpkin (a silky ganache of rich white chocolate, pumpkin, ginger, cloves, and cinnamon) and Double-Dark Basil, plus truffles like spicy Thai Peanut and Rum & Lemon Curd. *Roscar.com* or 512-303-1500.

ROYERS ROUND TOP CAFÉ, Round Top: Exceptional pies (especially the buttermilk and pecan), beautifully presented and perfectly packed. *RoyersRoundTopCafe.com* or 979-249-3611.

SUSIE'S SOUTH FORTY CONFECTIONS, Midland: Handmade white chocolate–coated "Texas Trash" in fun white bins plus tasty toffee. *SusiesSouthForty.com* or 800-221-4442.

THE TEXAS SAMPLER, Granbury: Dr Pepper goodies including ice-cream toppings, bottled Dublin drinks, and cake mixes plus Durham's nut collections from the Ellis Pecan Co. *TexasSamplerFoods.com* or 817-573-3486.

THREE BROTHERS BAKERY, Houston: Pecan pie, chocolate-pecan pie, and apple pies are yumsy, as is their beautifully twirled cinnamon coffee ring. Savor festive gingerbread people for the holidays. *3BrothersBakery.com* or 713-666-2253.

WISEMAN HOUSE CHOCOLATES, Hico: Sumptuous truffles made from exquisite chocolate, beautifully packaged. *WisemanHouse Chocolates.com* or 866-460-3571.

Sources

It's so easy now to jump online and find whatever ingredient or tool you need. Here are a few ideas:

ANCHO CHILE POWDER Find this at your local grocery or gourmet market or online at the Spice Barn or Penzeys. ★ *SpiceBarn.com, Penzeys.com*

BONNE MAMAN PRESERVES Available at most large or gourmet markets as well as online. ★ *WorldFiner.com*

CACAO NIBS Check gourmet grocers, health food stores, and online. ★ *Vitacost.com, KingArthurFlour.com*

CHEESECAKE PANS I like Norpro nonstick small cheesecake pans. Find them on Amazon. ★ *Amazon.com*

CHOCOLATE CHIPPER This is great for breaking ice, creating decorative hole patterns on cookies, and letting glazes seep into tres leches cakes. Find it on Amazon and at restaurant supply stores and gourmet markets. ★ *Amazon.com*

COCONUT OIL This is available at many health food and gourmet markets. It also can be found online at a number of vendors, with the best variety available from Amazon. Two recommended brands are Nature's Way Pure Extra Virgin Organic Coconut Oil and Barlean's Organic Extra Virgin Coconut Oil. ★ *Amazon.com*

COLA SYRUP I like to use the Baar brand. Available at many natural food markets and online. ★ *Amazon.com*

DESSERT DECORATOR PRO Great for dressing up any kind of cake, cupcake, or pie. Wilton has a good one. ★ *Wilton.com*

DIM SUM STEAMER This company sells a commercial-grade steamer that works for tamales. ★ *Katom.com*

DUBLIN DR PEPPER Find at gourmet markets and online via companies like Beverages Direct. ★ *BeveragesDirect.com, OldDocs.com*

ESPRESSO POWDER Available at Williams-Sonoma. ★ *Williams-Sonoma.com*

FIESTAWARE The Texas Cooking Fiestaware store can be accessed online. ★ *TexasCooking.com/fiestaware*

GUITTARD UNSWEETENED ROUGE RED DUTCH PROCESS COCOA POWDER Found at gourmet groceries and where fine chocolate is sold and online. ★ *Amazon.com*

HEART PIE PRESS I found mine at Martha By Mail. It's out of production, but it might be found on eBay from such sellers as "specialthingsz" by searching for "heart pie press pastry cutter Martha Stewart Mail" or on Amazon. ★ *eBay.com, Amazon.com*

SIFTED PASTRY FLOUR Texas's own Homestead Gristmill, in Waco offers a delightful product. ★ *Homestead-Gristmill.com*

TAMALE STEAMERS These can be purchased at Latino grocers and through numerous online sources. A good overview to choosing a steamer can be found at *Hispanic-Culture-Online.com/tamale-steamer.html*. ★ *MexGrocer.com*

VANILLA BEAN PASTE Find this at gourmet cooking shops and online. ★ *Amazon.com*

Permissions

MAMA MARION'S MANDELBROIDT (page 14) used with permission from Three Brothers Bakery. CHOCOLATE-PEANUT CLUSTERS (page 18) used with permission from Melanie Loving. CRAN-PISTACHIO COOKIES (page 19) used with permission from Kim McInnis. JENAY'S FAMOUS LEMON BARS (page 22) used with permission by its creator, Jenay Benge. THE MANSION ON TURTLE CREEK RASPBERRY BROWNIES (page 25), developed by pastry chef Nicolas Blouin, and photograph (page 26) used with permission by Rosewood Mansion on Turtle Creek. COCONUT DREAM PIE (page 31) used with permission from Shawn Horne. Photograph of SWEET POTATO QUEEN (page 39) Drew Danielle Henson-Hill, by Ruel Felipe, used with permission from the East Texas Jamboree. Photographs of DEEP-FRIED COKE, BIG TEX, and ABEL GONZALES (pages 43-45), taken by Kevin Brown, used with permission from the State Fair of Texas. TEXAS TWISTER (CHOCOLATE-ORANGE) MARSHMALLOWS (page 46) used with permission by its creator, Rachael Companik. MARIANO'S ORIGINAL MARGARITA MACHINE (page 55) photograph used with permission from the Smithsonian Institution. KERBEY LANE'S GINGERBREAD PANCAKES (page 60) used with permission by its creator, Kerbey Lane Cafe. APRICOT KOLACHES (page 63) used with permission by its creator, Little Czech Bakery. THREADGILL'S PECAN PIE (page 69) used with permission from Eddie Wilson of Threadgill's. BUD'S ROUND TOP BUTTERMILK PIE (page 73) used with permission from Bud Royer/Royers Round Top Café. BUMBLEBERRY CUTIE PIES (page 74) used with permission of its creator, "The Pie Queen" Jaynie Buckingham. TEXAS BIG HAIRS (page 77) used with permission by its creator, Rebecca Rather. GERMAN CHOCOLATE CARROT CAKE (page 82) used with permission of its creator, Arlene Lightsey. 1886 CHOCOLATE CAKE and historic photograph of THE DRISKILL HOTEL (page 84) used with permission from the Driskill Hotel. ANCHO-CHOCO TRUFFLES (page 90) by the late Jean Andrews used with permission from her family. ALMOND FLAN À LA FONDA SAN MIGUEL (page 94) used with permission by its creator, Chef Miguel Ravago.

VINTAGE BLUEBELL ICE CREAM photographs (pages 96 and 100) used with permission from Blue Bell Creameries. Vintage image of BIG RED BIRTHDAY PARTY (page 102) used with permission from Big Red, Inc. LUBY'S CHOCOLATE ICEBOX PIE (page 124) used with permission by its creator, Luby's Inc. THE STRANGE FAMILY'S CARAMEL-APPLE CAKE (page 130) used with permission by Catering by Don Strange of Texas. PUT THE LIME IN THE COCONUT CAKE (page 132) used with permission by its creator, Doreen Haller-Howarth. SEN. ZAFFIRINI'S PRALINE PECANS (page 139) and family photograph (facing page) used with permission by Senator Judith Zaffirini. HATCH CHILE AND AVOCADO ICE CREAM (page 142) used with permission of its creator, Adele Williams of San Antonio. HOMEMADE FUNNEL CAKES WITH SPIKED WHIPPED CREAM (page 149) used with permission by its creator, Jon Bonnell. SPICY CHOCOLATE-PEPITA COOKIES (page 151) and photograph of THE FOOD SHARK (page 152) used with permission from Krista Steinhauer and Adam Bork. LAURA BUSH'S COWBOY COOKIES (page 154) used with permission from former First Lady Laura Bush. ALMOND LACE COOKIES (page 157) used with permission from Noelle Bledsoe. DUTCH OVEN COBBLER WITH BUTTERMILK-LIME ICE CREAM (page 159) used with permission by its creator, Grady Spears. DEEP CHOCOLATE MERINGUE PIE (page 165) used with permission from Steve Labinski/TexasCooking.com. PERINI RANCH STRAWBERRY SHORTCAKES (page 170) used with permission by its creator, Tom Perini. GRANDMOTHER SHAUGHNESSY'S LEMON SPONGE CAKE (page 180) used with permission from Katherine Shaughnessy. BABE'S BANANA CAKE WITH CREAMY NUT FROSTING (page 182) and family photograph (page 2) used with permission from Kathleen Tibbetts. WATERMELON SOUP OOH LA LAH (page 195) used with permission by its creator, Ellise Pierce. MEXICAN DRESS COOKIES photograph (page 198) taken by Brianna Burnett, used with permission from Lily's Cookies.

Index

Table of Equivalents

The exact equivalents in the following tables have been rounded for convenience.

LIQUID/DRY MEASUREMENTS

U.S.	Metric
¼ teaspoon	1.25 milliliters
½ teaspoon	2.5 milliliters
1 teaspoon	5 milliliters
1 tablespoon (3 teaspoons)	15 milliliters
1 fluid ounce (2 tablespoons)	30 milliliters
¼ cup	60 milliliters
⅓ cup	80 milliliters
½ cup	120 milliliters
1 cup	240 milliliters
1 pint (2 cups)	480 milliliters
1 quart (4 cups, 32 ounces)	960 milliliters
1 gallon (4 quarts)	3.84 liters
1 ounce (by weight)	28 grams
1 pound	448 grams
2.2 pounds	1 kilogram

LENGTHS

U.S.	Metric
⅛ inch	3 millimeters
¼ inch	6 millimeters
½ inch	12 millimeters
1 inch	2.5 centimeters

OVEN TEMPERATURE

Fahrenheit	Celsius	Gas
250	120	½
275	140	1
300	150	2
325	160	3
350	180	4
375	190	5
400	200	6
425	220	7
450	230	8
475	240	9
500	260	10